SOCIAL SECURITY DISABILITY

REVEALED

Why it's so hard to access benefits
and what you can do about it

Spencer Bishins

Social Security Disability Revealed:
Why it's so hard to access benefits and what you can do about it

Written by: Spencer Bishins
Edited by: Allison Bishins

The information presented in this book is not legal advice.
It is for educational purposes only.
No attorney/client relationship exists between the author and the reader.
Anyone who requires legal advice should contact an attorney.

The examples in this book are fictitious. Any similarity to real life
situations is coincidental and not intended by the author.

No part of this book may be used or reproduced in any manner whatsoever,
without express written permission from the author,
except for brief quotations in book reviews or articles.

Printed in the United States of America

Table of Contents

PART 1: An Introduction to Social Security Disability

1. Why I Decided to Write This Book

I graduated from law school in the mid-2000s. During law school, I wanted to go into criminal law, representing people who are accused of committing crimes. There were motions, trials, and appeals, and it all seemed so fast paced and exciting! Then came the 2008 economic downturn. I was admitted to the Bar in April, but by September, it became clear that finding a job was going to be very difficult. With my new wife and I both having significant student loans, my dream job morphed into, well, the kind of job that involved a weekly paycheck.

For two years, I floated around in the unstable and unsettling world of legal document review. Basically, a law firm would hire me at an hourly rate, with no benefits, and could let me go at any time, for any or no reason. And I do mean at any time. During one project, at 10:00 am we were told there would be 40 hours per week plus overtime, and by 2:00 pm, all the attorneys were told the project had ended and our services were no longer necessary. But when the projects came, they often came with 60 hour weeks (meaning 20 hours of overtime) and nice fat paychecks. Plus, I had no other options. Law firms all around the country were scaling back. So, I, along with a lot of seasoned attorneys, did this work for as long as I had to.

My big break came when I was hired by the Social Security Administration (SSA), a federal agency, as an Attorney Advisor in 2010, thanks to the American Recovery and Reinvestment Act. The job posting stated that I would be reviewing disability cases. I presumed this meant that Social Security had some sort of disability program, but I had never heard of it. I did a bit of research to understand the process. I wanted to learn how a person applies for

2

disability, how to qualify, and how SSA determines whether a person is disabled.

From that time until the time when I left SSA over a decade later, I was involved in over 5,000 disability cases, writing or reviewing the ultimate decision for each case. I will save you from having to do the math. If there are 250 workdays in a year (and for me there were fewer, since federal employees get 11 holidays each year, and also a generous amount of sick and annual leave), in 10 years I would have served for around 2,500 workdays. This means I completed an average of two cases each day. Many of these cases had thousands of pages of medical evidence to review, and the average case included 600 to 800 pages of evidence. This evidence included bloodwork, imaging studies, doctor's reports, mental health treatment notes, as well as highly repetitive and disorganized treatment notes from clinics associated with the United States Department of Veteran's Affairs (the VA).

At this point, I hope you are thinking, "How could anyone possibly review that much detailed medical evidence *and* write or review a final agency decision in just four hours?" The answer is, poorly. I was excited to be a government lawyer engaged in the noble profession of public service. But the job I thought I was hired for was not the job I ended up doing.

SSA receives around two million applications each year for disability benefits. At one point during my career, more than a million people were waiting for a hearing with an Administrative Law Judge (ALJ). As a result, staff were told to go faster, write less, and spend less time on each case. But staff were also told to conduct a thorough review of all medical evidence, and then write a complete and legally sufficient decision that can withstand a legal challenge in Federal Court. Do you see the problem here?

3

SSA tells Congress they are conducting a fair, honest, and impartial review of applications for disability benefits. These are benefits that every worker who qualifies is entitled to after paying a Social Security tax for many years. When I started working as a lawyer, I was paying that tax too, but I never looked at my paystub closely enough to see what that tax was for. If you are an employee of a company, any company in the United States, look at your more recent paystub. Find the line that says *OASDI*. This is your Social Security tax. *OASDI* stands for Old-Age, Survivors, and Disability insurance. In other words, retirement, life insurance, and disability insurance. This means you too have paid into this system, even if you did not know you did.

Almost all of us are required to pay into the system. We get a job, we get a paycheck, and our employer's payroll provider automatically withholds the tax money and sends it to SSA. Each year, millions of people find they are unable to work because of a physical injury, a chronic condition, a sudden accident, a mental health condition, or often a combination of these factors. Many people do not know they have been paying into a national insurance program that is supposed to be there for them, if at some point during their lives they need it. But it is there, and a lot of people need it!

Unfortunately, however, the system is not set up for the people who need it. The system is set up to appease members of Congress, advance the careers of SSA employees, provide people with lots of holidays and leave, and provide a federal pension at retirement. In other words, SSA, which is supposed to prioritize the taxpayers, doesn't.

You deserve to know the truth. After you file your application for disability benefits, what really happens behind the scenes? How long does each person spend looking at your case? How much time is spent writing and reviewing the decision? What are the true motivations of SSA employees involved in this process? Does it help to have a lawyer representing you? Is the outcome of your case predetermined? What can you do to make things go more smoothly? Is there any hope of improving the process?

2. How I Hope You Will Use This Book

This book is not intended to be a self-help guide. I do not encourage anyone to DIY the Social Security Disability process. As you will see, the rules and regulations governing the program are simply too extensive, confusing, and legalistic. You need to have a qualified, experienced representative who can lead you through the process. The material I will present throughout this book is not a substitute for such knowledge and experience. It is intended to be an introduction to the Social Security Disability process, while also telling you what I have observed, and what I know to be true, even if SSA would never admit to some of what I will discuss. I would like to note that the terms I use throughout this book are terms provided to me during SSA trainings, as well as terms I used throughout my career as an SSA employee.

I intend for this book to be read by claimants, anyone considering filing a claim, and friends or family of a claimant or potential claimant. Counselors, medical professionals, claimant representatives, and anyone who runs, works with, or volunteers for an organization that helps vulnerable persons within the United States may also find benefit from the guidance I will present in this book. Anyone who has a physical or mental health condition and sometimes finds it difficult to work or make ends meet may find the information helpful as well. In other words, this is a book for everyone living in the United States and paying taxes to the United States government. Even if you don't work, this book is for you as well, since you are likely not working due to a physical or mental impairment, or a combination of impairments.

If you are a potential claimant: I recommend that you read this book, and then keep it to use as a reference as you move through the Social Security Disability process. You will want to refer back many times, re-reading sections that apply to where you are in the process. And of course, you need to find a representative. After reading this book, you will know more than almost all of your representative's other clients. You will be able to present an informed case to your representative, and you will be able to ask relevant questions. You will be an active participant in the preparation and presentation of your case.

If you are a current claimant: How this book can help you depends on where you are in the process, and also whether you have had a representative along the way. Everything I said in the prior paragraph applies to you too. If you have a hearing scheduled, it isn't too late to get a representative. You can even walk into your first hearing and tell the Judge you need more time to get a representative, and the Judge will most likely grant you one postponement for that purpose. If you received an unfavorable decision, you can hire a representative for the appeal, and some representatives will agree to step in at that point in the process with the hope of getting the case sent back for a new hearing. Don't give up! Educate yourself and then speak with a representative about your options.

If you are a friend or family member of a claimant or potential claimant: This book will still be helpful to you, even if the claimant doesn't read it. You can provide the claimant guidance, you can help get their medical records organized, and you can help the person find a good, caring representative. You can provide support for the claimant, and if you think the claimant cannot manage benefits in their own best interest, you could apply to serve as a "representative payee" who can help manage any benefits the claimant is awarded.

If you are a service provider or caregiver of a claimant or potential claimant, or if you run, work with, or volunteer for an organization that helps vulnerable persons: This book will help you speak to and relate to your patients/clients who may be Social Security Disability claimants. It will help you know what questions to ask your patient/client, and it will help you organize any records you keep for that person. These might be medical records, but they might also be reports of the person's living situation. Knowing the challenges that your patient/client will face as a Social Security Disability claimant will help you understand what that person is going through and how you can help.

If you are a claimant representative: While you obviously know the Social Security Disability system and the five-step sequential evaluation process, I do think you will find some benefit from the remainder of the book. Most representatives have not worked in a hearing office, or at the Appeals Council, so I hope that I can provide you some insight regarding how the cases are prepared for the hearing, how the decisions are made, how the written decisions are crafted, who does what within the hearing office, and why each party acts the way they do. I am also hoping that you may recommend this book to your clients, because having better informed clients who are active participants in this process will allow you to be a more effective representative.

3. Understanding Social Security Disability

The first thing you need to know is how the Social Security Administration (SSA) decides whether someone qualifies for disability benefits. This process is called the "five-step sequential evaluation process." It is called this because there are officially five steps to the process. Although, as I will explain later, there are actually six or seven steps. Those steps are always considered in the same order. Social Security regulations define disability as the inability to engage in "substantial gainful activity" (SGA) due to a medical impairment (or impairments), which can be physical or mental, for a period of at least 12 continuous months. The impairment(s) can also be expected to result in death, although this is a far less common scenario (for example, advanced-stage cancer).

Finally, the impairment(s) can be "expected to last" for a period of 12 continuous months, but in practical terms, because it takes most claimants a full year to get through the Social Security Disability process, this is the same as asking whether the impairment has already lasted for 12 months. In other words, at the time the claimant files the application, the claimant may allege that the impairment is, at that point, "expected to last" for 12 months. However, by the time the case actually gets to a Judge, 12 months would have likely passed. At that point, the Judge is looking back and asking whether the impairment "has lasted" for a period of at least 12 continuous months. The key takeaway here is that you have to be impacted for a full 12 months to be considered disabled under SSA regulations. This is called the "duration requirement."

Before we get into the five-step sequential evaluation process, we need to go over the two different Social Security Disability programs, because they are very different. The first program is an earned benefit. Some people might call this an "entitlement," which I think is an excellent term because when you pay into a program your entire working life, you have certainly earned those benefits, and that means you are very much entitled to receive them. This program goes by many names, and I use them interchangeably throughout this book. This program is outlined in Title 2 of the Social Security Act, so I may call these "Title 2" benefits. I may also call them "disability insurance benefits" because these are part of an insurance program, which I will describe shortly. They may also be called "Social Security Disability Insurance" benefits, or SSDI.

Title 2 benefits are earned simply by working, either as an employee or as an independent contractor. In both circumstances, you will pay a tax called the OASDI tax, which stands for Old-Age, Survivors, and Disability Insurance. This tax is essentially an insurance premium for the OASDI program. Almost every worker in the United States must pay this tax. Currently, the employee's portion of the OASDI tax is 6.2% of income, and the employer pays the same amount. Self-employed people do not have an employer, so they pay the entire 12.4%.

Some people will call this FICA, which stands for the Federal Insurance Contributions Act. However, FICA refers to the combined amount of both payroll taxes you see on your paystub: the OASDI tax and the Medicare tax. Currently, the employee's portion of the Medicare tax is 1.45% of income, and the employer pays the same amount. Self-employed people do not have an employer, so they pay the entire 2.9%. This means that if you are self-employed, you will pay both shares of both taxes. This is called the self-employment tax, and the grand total is 15.3% of your income. And that's *in addition to* your income tax! I will briefly discuss Medicare later. Medicare is a health insurance program that mostly serves people over the age of 65. However, a person found disabled and eligible for Title 2 benefits can become eligible for Medicare before age 65.

As you may already know, your OASDI tax payment covers you for retirement benefits. It also covers you for survivor's benefits, which is basically life insurance for your spouse or minor children if you die before retirement age. Finally, your OASDI tax payment covers you for disability benefits. As I said, almost all workers pay the tax, and that money is set aside and managed by the SSA trust fund. The money is used to pay benefits to retirees, to the spouses and minor children of a worker who has died, and to disabled workers. As this book is about the disability program, I will only focus on this last group.

But what about people who never paid the OASDI tax, such as stay-at-home parents who are not earning an income? What about part time workers, young people, and recent immigrants who have not worked long enough to be insured? There is a second program, called Supplemental Security Income (SSI), which is outlined in Title 16 of the Social Security Act. Why did we go from Title 2 to Title 16? Congress passed the Social Security Act that created the SSDI program in 1935, but did not create the SSI program until 37 years later, in 1972. Congress created this program to address people who are not eligible for SSDI. Unlike SSDI, SSI is *not* an insurance program. You will not pay an *SSI tax*. Instead, SSI is funded from general revenues, which means regular federal income taxes.

The SSI program is for people who have minimal income and few assets. Some might call this a *welfare* program, but I don't like that term because claimants must still qualify under the same standard of disability as for the Title 2 program. The difference is that for Title 2 benefits, the worker must be "insured," which I will discuss more below, whereas for SSI, there is no insurance. However, the SSI program has very strict income and asset limits. Many applicants who think they are under these limits often discover they are not.

There are other key differences between the SSDI and SSI programs. SSDI carries a five month waiting period, during which you will not receive any benefits. This waiting period is common with insurance programs. It's sometimes called an "elimination period." For example, if you have a private short term or long term disability policy, you likely must wait a certain amount of time before you can receive benefits, even for a covered situation. SSDI is similar. This waiting period starts on the first day of the month following when you are found disabled, unless you are found disabled on the first day of a month.

Here is an example to show how the waiting period is calculated. Let's say you were found disabled as of April 2nd. The five month clock would start on the first day of the next month, or May 1st. This means the waiting period would be May, June, July, August, and September, and you could receive your first monthly benefit payment (assuming you are found disabled and eligible for benefits) on October 1st. If, however, you are found disabled just one day earlier, on April 1st, then April counts as part of the waiting period. That means the waiting period would be April, May, June, July, and August, and your benefits could start on September 1st. Put more simply, only whole months are counted towards the five month waiting period. SSI has no waiting period, so you could get benefits on April 1st. But, if you are found disabled even the next day, April 2nd, you then must wait until the first day of the following month,

May 1st, for your first benefit payment. However, SSI has very strict income and asset limits, and the benefits for SSI are *much* lower.

There is another key difference between SSDI and SSI regarding healthcare. People who are eligible for SSI are usually eligible for Medicaid, a health insurance program for people with low income that is financed by a combination of state and federal funding. The income and asset limitations for Medicaid are similar to those for SSI. On the other hand, for SSDI, there are no income or asset limitations, because SSDI is an earned benefit. This means that Jeff Bezos could apply for SSDI because he pays the OASDI tax just like everyone else does. I have seen doctors who earned well over $200,000 per year apply for SSDI after serious medical conditions forced them to stop practicing medicine. Because they had significant assets, they would not be eligible for SSI, or Medicaid, but they remain eligible for SSDI benefits. For SSDI recipients, Medicaid is usually off the table, but SSDI recipients are instead eligible for Medicare.

That's right, some Medicare recipients are under age 65. Those Medicare recipients have been found disabled under the SSDI program. Eligibility for Medicare does not start until 30 months after the onset date of the disability, so you are on your own for medical care prior to that. However, Medicare will cover claims starting on the date of eligibility, even if you are found disabled after that time. For example, let's say a Judge finally finds you to be disabled three years, or 36 months, after your disability began. But you became eligible for Medicare after just 30 months, meaning your Medicare eligibility actually started six months before the decision was issued finding you disabled. You have been eligible for Medicare for six months, and yet you have been paying out-of-pocket for medical care during that time.

In this situation, the claimant can submit eligible medical claims from those six months of eligibility and get reimbursed by Medicare. Having Medicare coverage is a significant benefit, and to some claimants, it's even more valuable than the monthly disability benefit payments. Some claimants apply for SSDI benefits not even caring whether they get the actual monthly benefits, they just want Medicare coverage before age 65. For those claimants, going through this process is worth the hassle. But first, those claimants have to be found disabled using the five-step sequential evaluation process, which I will discuss in Part 2.

4. The Initial and Reconsideration Levels of Review

To fully understand my insider perspective on the Social Security Disability system, you must first understand how SSA wants you to believe the process works, and why it very much does not work that way at all.

Every case starts when a person files an application for Social Security Disability benefits (SSDI, SSI, or both), either online, by calling Social Security's 800 number, or by visiting a Social Security local field office and speaking to someone in person. Once this is done, another multi-stage process begins. Remember, this is the government, so there are a lot of abbreviations and processes.

There are multiple levels of review for a Social Security Disability case. The first level of review is at a state agency, usually the Department of Health in the claimant's state of residence. The application claim forms (SSDI, SSI, or both) and any evidence the claimant has submitted are reviewed by a state agency reviewer. This is a state employee who typically has a college degree and who earns around $40,000 per year. When making the initial determination in your case, the state agency reviewer will consult your medical records, but will also review the findings and medical opinions from two other sources.

The first source is a doctor called the "state agency medical consultant." You will never meet this doctor. This doctor will review all of your medical records and write a medical opinion regarding what you can do despite your impairments. This doctor may or may not have their own medical practice, and may or may not have substantial medical school loans. This person may be a new doctor (called a Resident), or may be a retired doctor who works part time reviewing Social Security cases. Whoever this doctor is, you can be sure the doctor's only goal is to get through as many cases as possible, as fast as possible, because SSA pays a flat fee per case. This means the more cases the doctor reviews, the more that doctor will be paid. As you can see, this process prioritizes speed over accuracy, a theme that will occur throughout this book.

If you state that there are physical and mental health impairments that prevent you from working, there may be two state agency medical consultants reviewing your medical records. One will be a medical doctor that will provide an opinion regarding your physical capabilities, and the other will be a psychiatrist or psychologist who will provide an opinion regarding your mental capabilities.

The second source is a doctor called the "consultative examiner." This is a doctor you will see in person. This will be a medical doctor if you say you cannot work due to physical impairments, or a psychiatrist or psychologist if you say you cannot work due to mental health impairments. If you allege inability to work due to both physical and mental health reasons, you will likely be sent to see two consultative examiners. Social Security will pay for these visits, and for any x-rays or other tests that these doctors perform. Again, SSA pays a flat fee per case, so these examinations will be very short. You can expect to spend around 10 minutes with a physical examiner and a little longer with a mental health examiner. After your visit, the consultative examiner will write a report describing what they saw and what they think you are capable of doing despite your impairments. This report will be sent to SSA, included in your medical record, and used to decide whether you are disabled.

Since these doctors get paid per case regardless of whether their opinions support an approval or a denial of your claim, this means they are impartial, right? Well, that depends on whether they want to keep reviewing Social Security Disability cases. If a doctor wants to keep getting assigned cases, the doctor needs to keep the state agency reviewing officials happy. As you will soon see, this means providing medical opinions that can be used to deny as many cases as possible.

Now let's turn back to the state agency reviewer, the one who has a college degree but is neither a doctor nor a lawyer, but who nevertheless reviews medical records and decides if they are legally sufficient to support a finding of disability. At this initial level, this reviewer typically finds around 30% of applicants to be disabled. At this point in the process, claimants rarely have someone representing them. However, there are many types of impairments and many circumstances that are slam dunk cases for the claimant and easy approvals for the state agency. This may be the person you pictured in your mind the first time I said the word *disabled*. You may have pictured a person who was involved in a car accident and who now cannot work due to being paralyzed, or because that person now has a traumatic brain injury.

In reality, such severe circumstances represent a small percentage of Social Security Disability cases. Most people who apply for disability benefits have a back disorder, a knee or shoulder impairment, anxiety, depression, fibromyalgia, diabetes, or another chronic condition that is not nearly as black and white as the impairments discussed above. This is the reason that around 70% of cases the state agency reviewer sees at the initial level are not approved. But why not just approve the other cases so people can get the benefits they need? Why would the state agency care whether someone qualifies for Social Security Disability benefits?

States, unlike the federal government, cannot run a budget deficit, so they are constantly looking for ways to save money. One of the largest portions of any state budget is the Medicaid program. Being denied disability benefits often forces people to return to work, which causes them to earn too much to qualify for Medicaid.

The point is that the state agency is not a neutral party. When a person's disability claim is denied at the initial level by the state agency reviewer, the state spends less on its Medicaid program. In my opinion, this means the state agency has a significant conflict of interest, which means it should not be involved in this process at all. Now you know the state agency reviewer is not as impartial as you thought. In fact, the opposite is true: there is a specific incentive to deny your claim.

This is why 70% of claims are denied at the initial level. The state politicians want to see most claims denied, so the state agency reviewing officials deny most claims. To do that, they need to have a medical opinion suggesting the claimant is not disabled to cite as the basis for denying the claim. The state agency medical consultant and consultative examiner doctors understand this, so they provide medical opinions suggesting that most people can work, and are therefore not disabled. These doctors provide the state agency reviewing officials with a steady supply of these opinions because they want to keep having cases sent their way for review. The doctors keep the state agency reviewing officials happy, which in turn keeps the state politicians happy. Everyone wins, except for the claimants.

The next level of review only applies in 40 of the 50 states. It is called reconsideration and it is a very similar procedure to the initial level of review. For this reason, over 95% of claims that get to the reconsideration level are denied, with the remainder involving new medical evidence that swayed the state agency reviewer. There are 10 states that bypass this level of review: Alabama, Alaska, parts of California, Colorado, Louisiana, Michigan, Missouri, New Hampshire, New York, and Pennsylvania. If you are in one of these states, after you receive the initial determination, your next step will be to appeal by asking for a hearing with a United States Administrative Law Judge (ALJ).

If your state includes the reconsideration level, you may be asked to see one or two more consultative examiners. Also, different state agency medical consultants and a different state level reviewer will review and decide the claim. However, the reviewers may very well be sitting in cubicles right next to each other, so this does not mean your case will receive any more of an honest and impartial review than it did during the initial review. The result is that for anyone not in one of the states listed above, a second denial at reconsideration is likely, and you will be headed to a hearing with an ALJ.

If the state reviewers are so biased, why does Social Security let them into the process? Well, if the state agency did not handle the first one or two levels of review, that would send a few million more cases each year to the hearing level, where an ALJ who works directly for SSA takes over the case. This would mean significantly expanding the size of SSA. Thousands more Judges would be needed, and possibly tens of thousands more support staff. The cost to the United States taxpayer would be tremendous. Members of Congress do not get elected by spending that kind of taxpayer money with no perceived benefit.

Of course, we are all paying for these services through state taxes, which come from a variety of sources. Oregon has an income tax and no sales tax. However, just across the bridge in Washington, it's the opposite, with a large sales tax but no income tax. In most states, the tax system lies somewhere in the middle of these extremes. Most people are used to adding sales tax to each purchase, so we don't notice an increase of a few cents at a time, like we do when federal taxes go up and our paychecks, therefore, go down.

This makes it much easier to shift these early levels of review to the states, who then have to help pay to administer the program. But as I said, the states have an interest in denying applications. So, the federal government is sending all of those cases to the states to do the initial and reconsideration reviews, but the states are then sending most of those cases back to the federal government. Cases are sent to the states, then back to the federal government, and tens of millions of dollars are spent in the process.

It would be more efficient to have one agency handle everything. Splitting the review duties between the state and federal governments costs a lot of money with no clear benefit. But none of us notice that this is happening, and that's the whole point. Politicians like it that way because then they don't need to justify the increasing costs of running the program.

As I said, most cases will eventually return to the federal level for a hearing with a United States Administrative Law Judge who works directly for SSA. I will delve into who those people are, how they are hired, and how the hearing level operates in Part 3. But first, I want you to understand that this is, ultimately, a legal process. In any legal proceeding, it is always a good idea to have a legal expert on your side. Therefore, I want to explain why you should not go any further in this process before you consult a representative. I do not benefit from you hiring a representative, but as you will see throughout this book, a representative is necessary to protect your rights, look out for your interests, and ensure the best possible outcome.

5. Why You Should Hire a Representative

Before we discuss the five-step sequential evaluation process or how the hearing level operates, we first need to discuss representation. After the initial and reconsideration (state agency) levels of review is when most people will hire a lawyer or non-attorney representative who is an expert on the Social Security Disability process. There are many reasons why someone typically hires an attorney at this point, not before, and not after.

The next step in the process involves an actual hearing with an Administrative Law Judge (ALJ). Most people, prior to this point, believe they are disabled. They think they will file a claim and quickly be approved. As discussed above, some people are approved by the state agency, but most are not. It can come as a real shock to be unable to work for an entire year because of serious medical impairments, only to be told your impairments are not significant and you can work a full time job.

This is an unpleasant surprise to most people, and it is also the first time they realize they are now in a fight with the United States government. They now realize the benefits they have paid for throughout their entire working lives are not automatic. They now realize that these benefits, which many people call *entitlements*, are something they are not automatically entitled to. They now realize this will be a long and exhausting process, and they need an expert on their side.

Fortunately, SSA does have a very supportive rule when it comes to getting a representative. You can hire a representative with no upfront fee! Hiring a representative is not required, and later I will discuss how ALJs treat claimants who are represented differently from claimants who are not. In Chapter 32, I will go

22

through a complex example showing how having a representative can mean the difference between being approved and being denied benefits. But for now, the point is that claimants are not legal experts. The Social Security rules and regulations are extensive and complicated, and they change frequently. For this reason, every claimant is better off having an expert who is on their side, and who will fight for the best possible outcome.

Almost all Social Security Disability representatives get paid the same way. But to explain that, I first need to explain the difference between past due benefits and ongoing, monthly benefits. The best way to do this is with an example. Let's say you applied for Title 16 benefits on January 1, 2018, alleging you became disabled on that same date. You are denied at the initial and reconsideration levels of review, so you hire a representative. You are then later approved on January 1, 2020, with your disability beginning on January 1, 2018.

You will receive ongoing SSI benefits every month from that point forward. But you will also receive SSI benefits for the two years when you were entitled to benefits but did not receive them (January 1, 2018, to January 1, 2020). Those are called "past due benefits" because they are for a period of time in the *past*, and you are now *due* to receive them because you have now been approved. Because those benefits are for a period of time in the past, the specific amount due is known. To make it simple, let's say your monthly benefit amount is $1,000. This means the past due benefits, for 24 months, are $24,000.

A representative will only receive a portion of these past due benefits. The representative will not be given any of the ongoing, future monthly benefits. Even better, the representative will only receive a very specific and limited portion of those past due benefits.

The representative is paid 25% of the past due benefits, capped at an amount set by Congress, currently $6,000. So, in our example, the past due benefits are $24,000, and 25% of that amount is exactly $6,000. That is the maximum amount the representative can earn, so if the past due benefits were any higher, the claimant would get 100% of the additional amount. If the past due benefits were only $20,000, the representative would only be able to get 25% of that lower amount, or $5,000. The other 75% of the past due benefits go to the claimant. In November 2022, the maximum fee a representative can earn will increase to $7,200. That is 25% of $28,800. If the past due benefits are less than this amount, the representative will receive 25%. If the past due benefits are more than this amount, the representative will receive the capped amount of $7,200.

The representative is paid directly by SSA from the claimant's past due benefits, before that money is sent to the claimant. A portion of the past due amount is simply withheld and sent directly to the representative. This way the representative does not have to worry about the claimant not paying, and the claimant does not have to worry about their attorney trying to collect any fees from them. The representative is paid automatically. It's a seamless way for the claimant to pay the representative.

All of this will be explained in a short document called a "fee agreement," which the representative will present to a prospective client to review and sign. This is required if the representative wants to receive the 25% payment directly from SSA, and most representatives do. The requirements for fee agreements are very strict. When a Judge issues a favorable decision, the Judge must also review and approve the fee agreement to make sure it complies with those rules. If the fee agreement is not done correctly, it will not be approved. In that case, the representative will have to file a "fee petition" with SSA, justifying why there should be a fee even though the fee agreement was not approved. That is a drawn-out process that most representatives prefer to avoid. It is easier for everyone to have the fee agreement approved by the Judge.

Within the fee agreement, you may also see a clause about costs. In addition to the 25% fee from past due benefits, representatives can collect a minimal amount for costs directly related to the representation. These include making photocopies, printing documents, and obtaining medical records, which may have a flat fee or a per page printing fee. However, the representative must explain in the fee agreement what costs will be assessed to the claimant. If you see reasonable, legitimate costs in your fee agreement, remember the representative is not making any money there. The representative is simply passing on to you the cost of preparing the case and securing your medical records. This must be disclosed in the fee agreement before any costs are incurred, and the representative should have receipts for any medical records that were obtained.

So, what do you get for your 25% of past due benefits? A representative can and will help you acquire medical evidence from your doctors, counselors, mental health practitioners, addiction treatment centers, the VA, etc. A representative can also contact former employers to obtain information about your work history. The representative also knows all of Social Security's complicated rules and regulations much more thoroughly than I can explain in this book. This person knows how the process works and how to present your case most favorably.

The other thing a representative can do is provide you with an honest review of your case, including telling you what your chances are of being approved. As you will see later in this book, not having someone by your side leaves you vulnerable to the whims, personality quirks, and misaligned incentives of SSA employees, including the ALJs.

For these reasons, I highly recommend that you hire a representative. But this person does not need to be an attorney. Many representatives are attorneys, but not all of them. The reason many representatives are attorneys is that attorneys can get automatically certified by SSA to receive direct payment. However, non-attorneys can also go through a certification process to represent claimants and get paid in the same way as attorneys.

Some people think they should avoid non-attorney representatives because they have no legal responsibility to act in the financial best interest of the claimant. This is untrue. Attorneys are regulated by the Bar Association in the state of their license, and are therefore subject to certain rules of professional responsibility. However, this does not mean that a non-attorney will act against your best interests. Non-attorney representatives do still have a professional responsibility to act in the claimant's best interest, which usually means in their financial interest. There is no reason to discriminate against a certified non-attorney representative simply because that person did not go to law school or sit for the Bar exam. I did these things, I am a licensed attorney, and I would hire a non-attorney representative if I felt that was the best person to present my case to the Judge.

Some representatives may act in their own best interest, rather than yours, but this has nothing to do with whether the person is an attorney. The representative gets paid the same fee for a favorable decision regardless of whether the person is an attorney.

Typically, the interests of the client and the representative will align and there will be no problem, but this is not always the case.

Here is an example to illustrate this point. The claimant is found disabled, but only as of the date of the hearing, with zero past due benefits. This means the attorney would get 25% of $0, meaning $0. The attorney worked hard on the case, but will not get a fee because there are no past due benefits. The claimant may be happy knowing there will be an ongoing monthly benefit moving forward. But the representative, wanting to try and get some past due benefits in order to collect a fee, may suggest appealing such a decision, telling the claimant they can fight for even more benefits.

In this case, there is a problem with that advice to appeal. This type of decision is called a "partially favorable" decision because there are two parts, a favorable portion and an unfavorable portion. There are two ways a decision can be partially favorable, and both have favorable and unfavorable aspects to them. First, the date disability starts can be found to be later than alleged by the claimant. In that case, the portion of the decision from when the claimant says disability began (the "alleged onset date" – AOD) until the date when the Judge finds the claimant became disabled (the "established onset date" – EOD) is unfavorable since the claimant was found not disabled during that time. Once the claimant is found disabled, the rest of the decision is favorable. This is called a "later onset" decision because the Judge finds that disability started, or "onset," later in time than the claimant alleged.

The other type of partially favorable decision is just the opposite. It is called a "closed period" decision. In such a decision, disability starts on the date alleged by the claimant (the AOD is also the EOD), so the favorable portion comes first. But then the Judge finds that at some point the claimant's disability ended, either because the claimant went back to work or because the claimant's medical conditions improved to the point that the claimant *can* go back to work. In a closed period decision, the unfavorable portion comes second. That portion is unfavorable to the claimant because the claimant has alleged that the disability continues, yet the Judge has said it stops.

When a claimant appeals a decision, the *entire* decision is appealed. So, if the representative suggests appealing a partially favorable decision, telling the claimant they can fight for more benefits, this is problematic because the favorable portion of the decision is also appealed. In such a situation, the incentives of the claimant and the representative no longer align. The claimant may want to keep the ongoing, monthly benefits while the representative may want to fight for past due benefits. This misalignment of incentives happens only when there is a later onset decision. The reason is that the representative needs past due benefits in order to collect a fee, and when the decision is a later onset decision, the past due benefits are reduced, or may even be zero.

The representative does not like having a reduced fee, and *really* wants to avoid a $0 fee, so the representative may want to appeal this type of decision. But, doing so also means appealing the favorable portion of the decision. The claimant may have been approved for ongoing, monthly benefits which could last many years, and could also be eligible for Medicare. All of that would be put at risk if the claimant appeals. This is a big decision for the claimant because there is a lot to risk for potentially very little gain.

An unscrupulous representative may try to convince the claimant to risk these hard-won benefits, something which, as you can see, is in the interests of the representative, but very likely not in the interests of the claimant. It is a risk because if the decision is overturned, everything the claimant was granted by the decision disappears, and the claimant may never get those benefits back. So, the representative wants to appeal the decision, while the claimant wants to let it stay in place. Do you see how the interests of the claimant and the representative no longer align?

This situation can occur, so it's something you should be aware of. If you think this may be happening to you, talk to a friend or family member before you make any decisions. The representative, attorney or non-attorney, cannot do anything without your consent. It's your case, and ultimately it's your decision. The representative cannot appeal if you tell them not to. And again, this situation can occur regardless of whether the representative is an attorney. There are many good attorney and non-attorney representatives out there, but there are also some bad ones. Interview several and find someone who is right for you. Perhaps ask what their advice would be if you were to receive a partially favorable, later onset decision. If their fee ended up being $0, would they want you to appeal? Your representative should give you an honest answer.

Another question people often have is when to hire a representative. Many representatives will wait until you have received one or two denials (at the initial and reconsideration levels of review) before they agree to take the case. There may be more than one reason for this. The first thing that comes to mind is how the representative gets paid. Many people think the representative does not want to take the case early in the process when the past due benefits will be low, because less past due benefits means a smaller fee for the representative. In other words, the representative may be less interested in helping you in the early stages and more interested in extending the time between the AOD and the decision. This increases the size of the potential past due benefits, and therefore makes it more likely that the representative will get the full fee to which the representative is entitled. I understand why people assume this is the representative's motivation.

But I think many representatives have another reason for not wanting to get into the case until it reaches the hearing level. Perhaps the representative wants to give you the opportunity to win your case at a lower level and keep all the benefits for yourself, rather than handing over 25% of the past due benefits to someone who has not done a lot to help. The representative may also feel ineffective at such an early stage of the process, when there is no in person hearing and when the medical record is not well developed. Maybe the person does not feel that it's ethical to accept a fee at that point in the process. In short, if a perspective representative wants to wait to take your case, just ask why. A good representative should be able to effectively communicate with you and should honestly explain the reasoning behind that decision.

I would like to conclude this chapter by introducing you to a type of claim for which you will have difficulty finding representation. Some local government employees, like teachers, who pay into a pension, can avoid paying the OASDI tax because they have the pension serving their retirement needs. However, by opting out of paying the OASDI tax, they are also giving up their eligibility for SSDI benefits. These employees, though, do still pay the Medicare tax.

So, if they become disabled, they cannot apply for SSDI benefits, but they can try to secure Medicare coverage by filing a claim called a "Medicare Qualified Government Employee" (MQGE) claim. The purpose of an MQGE claim is only to obtain Medicare coverage. The claimant must be found disabled under all the same rules as if they had filed an SSDI claim. However, there will be no SSDI benefits, which means no monthly benefits and also no past due benefits. Since a representative cannot earn a fee based on past due benefits, it can be very difficult to find representation for an MQGE claim. If you have an MQGE claim, you may be able to find representation through a non-profit organization that specializes in handling unusual cases.

PART 2: The Five-Step Sequential Evaluation Process

6. Step Zero

Now that we have covered the difference between the two Social Security Disability programs, and covered how a case makes its way through the initial and reconsideration levels, let's talk about how the decision makers at those levels, and later the Administrative Law Judge (ALJ), decide whether you are disabled. The decision maker, whether it be a state agency reviewer or an ALJ, will use the "five-step sequential evaluation process," which is how all Social Security claims are decided.

Of course, being a government program, it may not surprise you to learn that there are actually seven steps to consider. But if you have only an SSI claim, there are just six steps. SSA recognizes Steps 1, 2, 3, 4, and 5, but does not number the other two steps. I will call these "Step Zero" and "Step 3.5" because of where they fit into the sequential evaluation process.

Before moving to the officially recognized Step 1, we have Step Zero, which involves a question that the Judge in your case needs to answer "yes" to before you can continue. This step only applies to SSDI claims. So, if you have only an SSI claim, you can skip this step, which means your claim only involves six steps, not seven. Still with me?

Do you remember when I indicated that a person must be "insured" to qualify for SSDI benefits? Well, Step Zero is where we determine whether a person is insured. There are two parts to being insured. You must be both *fully insured* and *insured at the time you are found disabled*. Being fully insured is a one-time thing. Once you become fully insured, you have that status for life, never losing that designation.

Before I explain how you become fully insured, I need to explain to you the concept of "quarter credits." This is how Social Security keeps track of the OASDI tax that you pay, and how that translates into benefits when you become disabled, or later when you retire. There are a maximum of four quarter credits available during the course of a calendar year. You earn a quarter credit by working, earning money, and paying the OASDI tax. But the amount you need to earn to get a quarter credit is surprisingly low. In 2022, you earn one quarter credit for every $1,510 earned.

Even better, it does not matter *when* you earn the credits. You do not need to earn a quarter credit in each quarter of the calendar year. Instead, credits are based on gross earnings. In other words, you get your first quarter credit when your gross earnings reach $1,510 in the year. When you reach $3,020 earned during the year, you get your second quarter credit, even if you earned that second $1,510 in January of that year. Once your earnings reach $4,530, you get the third quarter credit. To earn all four quarter credits, you need to earn $6,040 in a calendar year. If you earned this much in your very first paycheck of the year, then congratulations, you just earned all four quarter credits before Groundhog Day!

Now back to how SSA determines if someone is fully insured. For anyone over the age of 31, making this determination is simple. Earn 40 quarter credits in your life, which reflects a total of 10 years of work and earnings, and you will attain a fully insured status. This means that when you reach retirement age, you will qualify for retirement benefits. It also means your spouse or minor children will qualify for survivor benefits should you die before retirement age. But for this book, all you need to know is that one must be "fully insured" to qualify for Title 2 benefits.

For people under age 31, it's too complicated to discuss here. The reason is that young people have not had as much time to work and earn Social Security quarter credits, so SSA has a sliding scale. The younger you are, the fewer credits you need to be considered fully insured for a disability claim. If this is you, rest assured there is a formula for younger workers where fewer credits are required, but you will need to consult a qualified representative to talk about your specific situation. I will keep my explanations to workers over age 31, as this explanation is what applies to most claimants.

Being fully insured is not enough to be eligible for SSDI benefits. While fully insured is a status you gain and then have for life, there is another component that SSA considers, one which you can gain and lose throughout your life. In addition to being fully insured, you must also be insured at the time you are found disabled. Remember that SSDI benefits are insurance benefits. You must qualify for the insurance program to be eligible to receive these benefits. The fully insured part tells SSA that you worked *enough* time throughout your life to qualify for the program. But SSA also wants to know that you worked *recently enough* to qualify for the program.

In this insurance program, you can become insured by working and earning credits, but if you stop working and you stop earning credits, the insurance can end. Thus, for every worker, there is a "date last insured" (DLI), which means the date your insurance *would end* were you to stop working and therefore stop earning quarter credits. Everyone has a DLI, but as long as you keep working and earning quarter credits, that date keeps pushing itself into the future. If you do not stop working prior to retirement age, you will never catch up to that date, meaning you were insured your entire working life.

Here is how SSA determines that you have active insurance. You need to have earned a quarter credit during 20 of the *last* 40 quarters. This means SSA conducts a rolling analysis. As a new quarter credit is evaluated, the 41st oldest quarter credit drops out of consideration. If you earn four quarter credits for five years in a row, you will earn 20 credits. This means that even if you then stopped working, for the next 20 quarters (five years) of analysis, you would have at least 20 credits out of the 40 quarters being considered. After five years, the quarter credits you earned start to drop out of consideration, and you would no longer be insured for the purpose of an SSDI claim.

Put in simple terms, if you worked and earned all four quarter credits for five years in a row, then your DLI will be five years after you stop working. So, if you worked and earned all four quarter credits in 2016, 2017, 2018, 2019, and 2020, but you did not work starting in 2021, your DLI would be December 31, 2025. That date, five years after you stop working, is the date your insurance *would end* if you do not continue to earn quarter credits. But keep in mind this date moves! If you keep working and earning credits, the date will continue to move into the future. If you don't work in 2021, but you then earn all four quarter credits in 2022, your DLI would move one year into the future, to December 31, 2026. If you stop working again, your DLI will stop moving forward in time. Then, if you do not earn additional quarter credits, you would eventually catch up to the DLI, and then you would pass it. At that point, you are no longer insured.

So, if you stop working, and if you earn no quarter credits for 20 quarters (five years) in a row, you will reach the DLI, and then pass it. Once your DLI is in the past, you can still file a claim for SSDI benefits, but you would need to be found disabled *before* the

DLI. In other words, you need to be found disabled when you were insured. If you start working again, your DLI will start moving again, and if you work long enough, it will move into the future once again. SSA can tell you what your current DLI is, but you should also consult a qualified representative to make sure that information is accurate, especially if this is an issue that could keep you from getting SSDI benefits and/or Medicare. This is a very complicated calculation, especially for those with a sporadic work history.

For most people, the DLI will be December 31st of a particular year. If there are some years when you earned less than four quarter credits, your DLI may instead be March 31st, June 30th, or September 30th. It will always be one of these dates, which represent the end of the four quarters in the calendar year, because everything with Social Security is based on a quarterly system. So, if your DLI is March 31st and you earn one additional quarter credit, the DLI will move forward in time to June 30th. But the DLI will only ever be one of these four calendar dates.

Also, remember that you do not need to have a DLI in the future. It can be in the past, so long as it is *after* the date you say you became disabled. If the year is 2022, and your DLI is December 31, 2020, you need to be found disabled before December 31, 2020, to get SSDI benefits. If you say you became disabled in 2019, and if the Judge agrees, then you are fine, you were insured at the time you became disabled. Even if the Judge disagrees and finds you did not become disabled until December 1, 2020, you would still be approved for SSDI benefits because you are being found disabled at a time when you were insured.

But if the Judge thinks you did not become disabled until sometime in 2021, that's bad. No matter how severe your medical conditions became in 2021, if you are not insured at the time when you would be found disabled, then you do not qualify for SSDI benefits. It's an insurance program, and you must be insured. In the previous example, the Judge would simply find that you were not disabled as of December 31, 2020, the DLI, and would not analyze any evidence after that point.

Calculating the DLI is very complicated, but SSA has an excellent system for doing so and for keeping track of the DLI of every worker. But again, a skilled, knowledgeable, and experienced representative may want to confirm your DLI manually by reviewing your Social Security quarter credit history. This is particularly important if your disability began around the time of your DLI. Your application needs to state that you became disabled before the DLI, when you had insurance, or you will not have a valid SSDI claim. This is what lawyers call a *threshold* issue. It means that if you were not fully insured or your disability did not begin before the DLI, you are completely ineligible for SSDI benefits. In such a circumstance, the sequential evaluation process would end even before reaching Step 1.

7. Step 1

If your claim is for SSI only, Step 1 will be the first thing the Judge will consider. If your claim is SSDI, and if you are both fully insured and your DLI is after the date you say you became disabled (known as the "alleged onset date" or AOD), Step 1 will be the next step in the process.

Before even asking what medical impairments prevent you from working, the Judge must first decide whether you are engaging in "Substantial Gainful Activity" (SGA). The definition of disability starts by asking whether the person has an inability to engage in SGA due to a medical impairment or a combination of impairments. Thus, if the person can engage in SGA, that person is not disabled under SSA regulations. This is why the Judge will decide whether you have engaged in SGA before evaluating your medical conditions.

Now, you might be thinking, "But I was not engaged in *substantial* gainful activity even when I was working. I didn't earn that much. It certainly was not *substantial*." The average worker in the United States earns somewhere around $40,000 per year (before taxes) working around 40 hours per week. If we use 50 weeks per year to keep the calculation simple, this means this person earns $40,000 for working 2,000 hours. I know, you probably work more than 40 hours per week, and maybe you don't even get two weeks off throughout the year, but the math is simpler this way.

If we take $40,000 per year, and we divide by 2,000 hours per year, we have a wage of $20 per hour. For this illustration, we won't talk about benefits, paid time off, or holidays. Again, let's keep this simple. Let's just assume our average worker earns $20 per hour, and then develops a medical impairment that makes it difficult to work. How do we determine whether this person was engaged in *substantial* gainful activity?

The Social Security Administration has a specific definition for what is considered SGA. For this purpose, it uses a monthly income figure, not an hourly figure. So, let's go back to the annual income of $40,000 and divide by 12 months. That gives us a monthly income of around $3,333. Is that SGA? The answer is yes, it is in fact *far above* the SSA standard for SGA. In 2022, a person who does not have a vision impairment (there is a different calculation for persons with vision impairments) is considered to have performed SGA when that person has earned just $1,350 in a month.

Yup, that's all. $1,350 per month (before taxes). Because some months have four weeks and some have five, SSA presumes there are 4.333 weeks per month. This makes sense, since a quarter of a year is 13 weeks, but only three months. If we take $1,350 and we divide by 4.333, we have a weekly income of around $312. If we then divide by 40 hours per week, we arrive at an hourly rate of just $7.80 per hour. This means SSA considers you to be able to perform *substantial* gainful activity if you are earning just above the federal minimum wage (which has been $7.25 since 2009), but *below* the minimum wage in the majority of states, while working a full time, 40 hour per week schedule. You probably would not consider $7.80 per hour to be *substantial*, but SSA does.

In other words, when asking if you are performing *substantial* gainful activity, what SSA is really asking is whether you can work on a full time basis, or whether you can at least earn the same amount of money in a month *as if* you worked a full time schedule at just above the federal minimum wage. It's the dollar amount that counts, not the number of hours you can work. SSA

40

does not actually care how many hours you can work, what they care about is whether you can earn the *equivalent of* a full time work schedule right around the federal minimum wage.

So, let's now consider a lawyer (like me) who earns $200 per hour (unlike me). The lawyer starts work at 9:00 am on Monday, April 1st. At that hourly rate, the lawyer needs to work 6.75 hours to reach $1,350. This means that even with a lunch break and two other smaller breaks, by 5:00 pm the same day, before the end of the first day of the month, the lawyer has already earned enough to have met the SGA standard for that month.

Now let's say the lawyer becomes impaired and files a disability claim, but the lawyer is still able to work two hours each week, or eight hours per month. At $200 per hour, the lawyer is still earning $1,600. This is SGA, so the person's disability claim will be denied even though the person's income has dropped from $400,000 per year to less than $20,000. SSA does not care what you *used* to earn, or what you *would like* to earn. All that matters is whether you are earning above the SGA amount each month.

The SGA calculation is different for self-employed persons. Those workers pay the self-employment tax (OASDI tax plus Medicare tax) based on their net profit (revenues minus expenses). Net profit is also the figure used by SSA to calculate SGA. So, if you are self-employed and you earned $10,000 in a month, but your expenses were $9,000, your net profit is just $1,000, which would not be considered SGA. However, there are several additional tests to determine SGA for self-employed individuals. If you are self-employed, you need to consult a representative to assess your particular situation.

Confusingly, not all work done at the SGA level prior to your hearing will count as SGA. The reason is that the agency wants to encourage you to try and go back to work. Therefore, you can try going back to work and earn over the SGA amount. If the work ends or your earnings dip below the SGA level within six months, this may be considered an "Unsuccessful Work Attempt" (UWA). If you cannot sustain that work activity because of your impairment(s), or because the job involved special conditions related to your impairment that were taken away, the Judge can decide this is a UWA. In that situation, the work attempt will not disrupt your 12 continuous months under SGA.

To be a UWA, the job must have ended because of your impairment(s), or because of the removal of special conditions related to your impairment, not just because business was slow or you didn't like your job. Here is an example to illustrate a UWA. Let's say you worked as a cashier and you have a knee impairment that makes it painful to stand. Due to pain, you worked below the SGA level for five months. Then, your employer obtained a stool so you could sit, which allowed you to work more. Your earnings were at the SGA level for five months. Then, your employer took away the stool for you to sit on while you worked. The removal of that special condition caused you to have to quit that job, and you did not work for the next five months prior to filing a disability application.

Is there a continuous period of 12 months when you did not work due to your impairment? If the Judge decides the work you did at the SGA level was a UWA, then you did not work at the SGA level for 15 months. This is because any work performed during a UWA does not prevent a finding of disability. Therefore, you would have a 15 month period of being unable to do work at the SGA level because of your impairments, which satisfies the 12 month duration requirement.

But a claimant needs to be very careful to not work over the SGA level unless it is truly an attempt to return to work. The reason is that there is a six month limit for a UWA, and also you will need to prove the work ended due to your impairment(s) or the removal of special conditions. If you cannot do that, or if you work longer than six months, it will not be a UWA and your disability application will be denied at Step 1 of the sequential evaluation process for engaging in SGA.

Practically, the SGA rule means that a person must earn next to nothing, or just nothing, to be eligible for disability benefits. And remember, this has to remain the case for a continuous period of 12 months. In other words, to even be considered for a benefit that you have paid a tax for your entire working life, you essentially need to be nearly destitute. You can work part time and be paid under the SGA amount, and still earn enough during the course of a calendar year to receive all four quarter credits. However, most people working just part time can barely pay rent and buy food, let alone pay for expensive health insurance and even more expensive medical care.

As we will see later, this is one of the most significant problems with our current disability system. SSA requires claimants to have almost no income, and yet penalizes someone for not seeking sufficient medical care, even if that person was not seeking care because, with almost no income, they could not afford it. No wonder SSA finds that so many people don't have sufficient medical evidence to prove they are disabled! I'll discuss this more in Chapter 31.

8. Step 2

The next step in the sequential evaluation process is whether the claimant has a "severe impairment." The first time I heard this term in my SSA training class, I again pictured a person sitting in a wheelchair, with no functional use of the legs. Now *that* is a severe impairment! But SSA simply defines severe impairment as an impairment that more than minimally impacts one or more basic work activities. These activities involve the abilities and aptitudes necessary to do most jobs, and they include: walking, standing, sitting, lifting, pushing, pulling, reaching, carrying, handling, seeing, hearing, and speaking. These activities further include understanding, remembering, and carrying out simple instructions; making simple judgments; responding appropriately to supervision, co-workers, and usual work situations; and dealing with changes in a routine work setting.

So, SSA considers *any* physical or mental impairment that more than minimally impacts *any* of these activities for a period of 12 months to be severe. For example, when I was a child, I had asthma. I sometimes had difficulty breathing, which could make it hard to walk long distances without taking breaks. These symptoms lasted for several years. According to SSA regulations, I had a severe impairment because I had a medical impairment that more than minimally impacted my ability to walk, and this impact lasted more than 12 continuous months.

Does this mean I was disabled? No. Remember, there are additional steps in the sequential evaluation process. But it does mean that I had what SSA calls a severe impairment. In legal terms, we call this a *de minimus* test. In English, think minimal, as in there is a very minimal threshold for showing that someone has a severe impairment at Step 2. As long as you have some medical evidence during the period at issue in your case, it will not be difficult to get past this step. It's something to be aware of, but most claims are not denied at Step 2.

Many claimants, friends, and family members confuse the ability to work and the ability to engage in basic work activities. But the ability to do basic work activities and the ability to work are different concepts, and it's important to understand the difference. Someone may think, "My knee is busted, I had to have knee replacement surgery, and now I can't walk very well. I guess that means I can't work as a high school teacher anymore, since that job requires standing and walking around the classroom. I guess this must mean I'm disabled." This is a logical thought process, but this is not how SSA regulations work.

At Step 2, we are asking whether there is even a small limitation to a basic work activity. But even if the answer is yes, a person does have some sort of limitation in one or more of these areas of functioning (in other words, has some degree of difficulty with one or more basic work activities), this does not mean the person will be found disabled. As I said, it's fairly easy to get past this step, as it does not take much to convince the Judge that you have an impairment that limits one or more of those activities. The Judges understand that almost every claimant will have at least one impairment that limits at least one basic work activity.

But having limitations to basic work activities is not the same thing as being unable to work. Take the high school teacher example above. Perhaps that person cannot stand or walk for long, but could teach while sitting. Or perhaps that person has work experience doing a job that requires less standing or walking, such as being an office administrator. Maybe the person cannot do the teaching job at all, but could do other work that could be learned quickly, such as assembling eyeglasses or sorting nuts (yes, these are actual jobs that SSA uses to determine that someone can work). So, while this person has suffered a knee injury with a significant impact on the ability to stand and walk, and while he therefore has limitations in this specific activity, this is not the same thing as being unable to work. To make that determination, we need to move ahead with the sequential evaluation process.

9. Step 3

Step 3 is a step that is great for the claimant, because while a person can be approved at this step, one *cannot* be denied at this step! Originally, to be classified as disabled, the medical evidence needed to prove very specific elements. The elements differ for each impairment, and they can be found in the Code of Federal Regulations (CFR), along with all other federal regulations. Everything related to Social Security Disability is found at Title 20 of the CFR (Part 404 for SSDI regulations, and Part 416 for SSI regulations).

While this step is excellent for the claimant, unfortunately, most cases are not decided at Step 3 anymore. The reason is that these lists, referred to by SSA employees as the "listed impairments," or by an even shorter colloquial term, "the listings," are incredibly specific, and often the evidence will not be sufficient to prove every single element. If your evidence is specific enough to satisfy the strict requirements of a listing, congratulations! You will likely be approved quickly and with little difficulty. But almost all cases will move past this step and further along the sequential evaluation process.

If the specific listing criteria are not satisfied, you may have one more chance to have your claim approved at this step. The Judge can call a medical expert to testify at the hearing and say that the severity of your particular impairment(s) is *medically equivalent* to the severity described by a specific listing. A medical expert's confirmation is necessary for the Judge to make such a finding. I will discuss the medical expert's role at the hearing in Chapter 16.

Let's review where we now stand. For an SSDI claim, one must be fully insured and insured at the time disability begins. For all claims, one cannot be earning more than $1,350 per month, which means the person may not be able to afford food, rent, utilities, and likely cannot support a family. The person must therefore be essentially destitute, and yet must be able to provide sufficient medical evidence to show by a "preponderance of the evidence" (which means *more likely than not*) that the person has a medical impairment or impairments that prevents the ability to engage in SGA for a period of 12 continuous months.

The person must have at least one *severe* impairment, which we know is fairly easy to demonstrate. The impairment(s) need to have existed for at least 12 continuous months (or be likely to do so, or be likely to result in death). As we move forward in the sequential evaluation process, we will presume that the Judge did not find that any specific listing was met or confirmed as medically equivalent by a medical expert.

10. Step 3.5

At this point, we have a person who is not working, or not earning very much, and who has medical impairments that prevent the ability to work at the SGA level. So how do we know whether this person is disabled? By now you have read the Chapter title, so you know that Step 3 is not followed by Step 4. This is the government, nothing is simple. There is an unnumbered step between Steps 3 and 4, which I call Step 3.5. We cannot move on to Steps 4 and 5 without first doing this step.

At Step 4, SSA will decide whether you can do any of your past work, and if not, at Step 5, whether you can do other work that exists in significant numbers in the economy (which I will explain in Chapters 11 and 12). However, before Step 4, SSA must determine what it is you are capable of doing *despite* your impairments. Even though you have some medical conditions that cause some medical limitations, everyone remains capable of doing some things. The purpose of this step is to separate limitations from capabilities, and to decide what you remain capable of doing even with your various medical conditions. This is called the "Residual Functional Capacity" (RFC). We use the word "residual" because we are talking about what is left over in your mind and/or body after your impairment(s) impact you. "Functional capacity" is just a fancy way of saying "what you can do." Thus, the RFC is a determination of what you can do despite your impairments.

This is not a determination of what you can do on an average day, for a week, or even during an entire month. This is a determination of the *most* you are capable of doing for eight hours per day, five days per week, 40 hours per week, on an ongoing (which really means never-ending) basis. The Judge will go function-by-function, and determine how much you can do all of those work related activities previously discussed at Step 2: walking, standing, sitting, lifting, pushing, pulling, reaching, carrying, handling, seeing, hearing, and speaking; but also understanding, remembering, and carrying out simple instructions; making simple judgments; responding appropriately to supervision, co-workers, and usual work situations; and dealing with changes in a routine work setting.

It is important to remember that if you do not have a corresponding impairment, then nothing can, from the Judge's perspective, impair a particular capability. If you have a leg impairment, such as a knee injury, this cannot impact your ability to speak, to remember things, or to use your arms. This makes logical sense. But what is illogical is that the Judge starts from a place where every person is superhuman prior to having a medical impairment.

To illustrate what I mean, let's presume someone has anxiety and depression. These are mental impairments, so they cannot affect the person's ability to lift or carry objects. With no physical impairment, the Judge will find this person capable of doing heavy exertion work, which means lifting 100 pounds. Similarly, because these impairments do not impact the person's ability to stand or walk, the Judge will find the person can stand and walk for eight hours per workday. The key takeaway here is that unless you have an impairment in a particular body system, there cannot be a limitation in that area of functioning.

I worked a job where I was on my feet all day, and it was exhausting, even for a healthy, able-bodied person. I have never been able to lift 100 pounds on my own, and certainly not repetitively. In other words, SSA and its Judges presume you are

50

capable of being an Olympic weightlifter or speed walker unless you show them medical evidence to the contrary. However, in reality, an adult who is 5'2" tall and weighs 100 pounds, and who is perfectly healthy, will most likely not be capable of lifting that person's entire body weight, at least not safely. That is irrational, and yet it's what Social Security expects of you unless you have specific evidence to the contrary. Keep this in mind when thinking about the RFC and how it is used at Steps 4 and 5 of the sequential evaluation process.

As I explain Steps 4 and 5 below, it will help to use an example. I will start here, and I will continue by referencing this example as I explain Steps 4 and 5 in Chapters 11 and 12. In this example, we will consider a 48-year-old plumber who injured his back while working. Plumbers bend a lot. In SSA jargon, bending at the waist is called "stooping." Because plumbers bend and stoop a lot, back injuries are quite common. For simplicity, let's say there is no workers' compensation involved, as we will keep this only a Social Security Disability benefits claim. This person did not go to college, and has been working since graduating high school at age 18. He has worked for 30 years, first as an apprentice, and then as a fully licensed plumber.

SSA considers the plumber job to be medium exertional level work activity. There are four categories of exertional activity: heavy, medium, light, and sedentary. "Heavy" exertion jobs involve lifting up to 100 pounds, like construction worker or firefighter. "Medium" exertion jobs involve bending and stooping most of the day, like plumber, and they also involve jobs where a person has to lift up to 50 pounds, like someone who works in a pet store and has to lift 50 pound bags of dog food. "Light" exertion jobs involve standing or walking most of the day, like being a restaurant server, and they also involve jobs where a person has to lift up to 20 pounds, such as a grocery store clerk. Even if the clerk sits on a stool to scan groceries, the job is considered light exertion work because sometimes the clerk needs to lift a heavy item to scan it. The final category is "sedentary" exertion work, which are sitting jobs involving very little lifting or carrying, sitting most of the day, and significant use of the hands. An example of sedentary exertion work is receptionist, which involves typing, greeting people, and sorting mail, mostly while sitting.

Returning to our plumber, let's presume the Judge decides the medical evidence shows that this person can stand and walk without a problem, but he has a back injury that makes frequent bending very painful. We will presume that the claimant's impairment is well supported by medical evidence. Is the claimant disabled? To decide this, we need to proceed to Steps 4 and 5 of the sequential evaluation process. No claim is approved or denied at Step 3.5. This step is simply to decide the claimant's RFC, which is used to make a determination at Steps 4 and 5.

Steps 4 and 5 are not medical findings, they are vocational findings. For these steps, the Judge has already decided that the claimant has a severe impairment, and has already evaluated all of the claimant's impairments to determine all of the specific functional limitations that make up the RFC. So, when we get to Steps 4 and 5 of the sequential evaluation process, we will not be evaluating medical evidence anymore. Instead, we will be looking at evidence regarding the claimant's past work, and we will decide whether the claimant can go back to doing any of that past work, or whether the claimant could instead do other work that exists in significant numbers in the national economy.

11. Step 4

At Step 4, the Judge will decide whether the person can perform "past relevant work." This term has a very specific definition involving three elements. First, the work must have been performed at the SGA level. Second, it must have been performed during the past 15 years (the 15 years preceding the decision; but if the DLI is in the past, then the 15 years preceding the DLI). Third, it must have been performed long enough for the person to learn how to do the job to an average performance level. Thus, the *work* must be both *past* and *relevant*. What we are really doing at this step is telling a person, "Yes, you have impairments that somewhat limit you, but we see that you did this specific job before, and we think you can do it again." If the person can go back to doing work that was done in the recent past, then that person is not disabled.

Let's break down the elements. First, the work must have been done at the SGA level. How can we say that a person can *return* to do work at the SGA level if the person never worked and earned at that level to begin with? Accordingly, this is the first consideration. If a past job was not done at the SGA level (meaning the claimant earned an amount considered to be SGA), it will not be considered past relevant work.

Next, the work must have been done during the past 15 years. Anything older than 15 years is considered too old. Technology changes over time, so what a computer repair person did in 2007 will be very different from what that person does in 2022. Any skill learned before 2007 is too ancient to be considered relevant 15 years later. Also, work done more than 15 years in the past is considered too remote in time for the person to remember any skills that may have been obtained way back then. Accordingly, we only consider work done within the past 15 years, no matter the skill level involved. If the DLI is in the past, we go back 15 years from that date. For example, if it is 2022, but the DLI is December 31, 2019, we look at work the claimant did back to 2004. In such a situation, the Judge will not consider vocational evidence after the DLI in 2019. Thus, in order to consider a full 15 years of work history, we must go back 15 years from December 31, 2019.

The final element is a bit more complex. Even if the person did the job at the SGA level, and during the prior 15 years, we cannot expect someone to return to a job unless the person learned how to do that job adequately, meaning to an average performance level. This is particularly important if the job involved a high degree of skill. A person needs time to learn skills, and the more highly skilled a job is, the more time it takes to learn. It would not make logical sense to tell someone they can go back to doing a job when that person never did it long enough in the past to learn the necessary skills.

Now is a good time to return to the plumber example. Our plumber worked from age 18 to age 48, 30 years, so there is no question he would have learned all the necessary skills. But what if he did the job for one year, would that be enough? Maybe. What if the person did the job of plumber for just one month, 14 years ago, how about that? We need a way to determine the precise amount of time a person needs to have done a job in order to have learned to do it to an average performance level. This is called the "Specific Vocational Preparation" (SVP).

SSA regulations describe all jobs as unskilled, semi-skilled, or skilled. A job is unskilled when there is little or no judgment needed to do simple duties that can be learned on the job (SVP level 1 or 2). Semi-skilled work is work which involves some skills, but

54

which does not require doing more complex work duties (SVP level 3 or 4). Skilled work involves more skills, and also requires that the worker use judgment (SVP levels 5 through 9). Thus, the higher the SVP, the more highly skilled the work, and the longer it will take for a person to learn to do the job to an average performance level. Unskilled jobs can be learned in less than a month, while highly skilled jobs can take as long as 10 years to learn.

Being a plumber is considered a skilled job, with an SVP of 6. This means it takes one to two years to learn to do to an average performance level. That makes sense since people will often apprentice for that much time before becoming fully licensed plumbers. In our example, the plumber did the job for way more than that amount of time, during the past 15 years, and it was a full time job, so it was done at the SGA level. Therefore, SSA will consider the job to be past relevant work. This will likely be confirmed at the hearing by the vocational expert, who is an expert on all of the jobs in the entire national economy. The vocational expert knows what skills each job has, but also knows about all of the physical and mental demands of each job. The vocational expert is usually a job placement specialist who perhaps used to help people get jobs, but who now sits in the Social Security Disability office (or, more recently, at a desk at home) all day long and does nothing but testify at Social Security Disability hearings. We will discuss this person further in Chapter 17.

Step 4, however, is not yet complete. Once we determine what jobs are past relevant work, we need to then determine if a person with the claimant's RFC can do any of that past relevant work. Let's illustrate how this is done by returning to the plumber. If he had impairments, but he was able to bend without limitation, we might say he could return to his prior job as a plumber. However, in our case, he cannot bend often, which means he cannot do that job, since it requires a lot of bending. This would be confirmed at the hearing by the vocational expert, who would say that someone who cannot bend cannot do a job that involves bending. I know that seems obvious, but the Judge can only make a decision based on evidence, so the Judge must ask that simple question and get that simple answer from an expert witness for that information to officially be evidence in the case.

Once the plumber job is eliminated, we then need to see whether any other past jobs fit what the claimant can do. In this case, we only had one past job to consider, but often people will have several jobs during the past 15 years that are considered at Step 4. When that is the case, the Judge will consider each job individually, making sure it fits all the elements to be considered past relevant work. For each past job that qualifies as past relevant work, the Judge will then decide if a person with the claimant's RFC can do that past job. If the answer is yes for *any* past job, the person is not disabled, so the decision will be unfavorable.

Sometimes a person will have no jobs during the prior 15 years that satisfy all of the past relevant work requirements, in which case the Step 4 analysis will be very short. Other times, the Judge will move past this step quickly not because there are no jobs to consider, but because the Judge can see that a denial at Step 5 will be fairly easy to justify. Why spend a lot of time and effort analyzing several past jobs when you can breeze past that step and deny the person's claim more easily at Step 5? In Chapter 12, you will learn why a denial at Step 5 is often far easier for the Judge to justify than a denial at Step 4.

For our plumber, the only job to consider at Step 4 involves a lot of bending, and he can no longer bend often, so that job is eliminated. There are no other past jobs to consider, so we are done with Step 4. Unfortunately for our plumber, there is one more step. While claims can be approved or denied at Step 5, as we will see, not every claim that makes it that far has an equal chance of being approved. It turns out that our plumber never had a real chance of being approved for Social Security Disability benefits, he just doesn't know it yet.

12. Step 5

At Step 5, the Judge will decide whether the person can perform any other work that exists in significant numbers in the national economy. If the answer is yes, the person is not disabled. If the answer is no, the person is disabled. This step concludes the sequential evaluation process, so we need an answer one way or the other.

During my SSA training, I was particularly interested in this final step. How could we possibly know whether there is *any* work that exists in significant numbers in the national economy that a person can perform? How do we evaluate the entire national economy with over a hundred million jobs? The answer is: poorly. At this step, the Judge will once again call upon the services of the vocational expert. This expert is someone who is hired by SSA, and who is paid by SSA to testify, so you do not have to worry about finding one, the Judge's office will handle that.

To illustrate how the Judge will move through Step 5 of the sequential evaluation process, let's go back to our unfortunate plumber. He has a back condition that makes it difficult to bend, so he cannot continue being a plumber. At Step 5, the Judge needs to determine whether there is any "other work" (*other* meaning besides the claimant's past relevant work) that exists in significant numbers in the national economy that the claimant can perform.

The answer will be yes, there is other work. While the plumber's back disorder makes bending difficult, the Judge already knows there is other work the claimant can do. Because there is no limitation lifting, carrying, standing, or walking, there will surely be some light work or sedentary work this person can do. Because they know the SSA regulations well, both the Judge and the vocational expert knew this before the hearing even began.

Here is the formal procedure at Step 5 for gathering the evidence the Judge needs from the vocational expert. The Judge will pose a *hypothetical* scenario to the vocational expert. The Judge will invent a hypothetical person and assign that person work related limitations that match the claimant's impairments and difficulties. The scenario will likely have limitations that are close to what the Judge intends to put into the RFC in the decision. The Judge will then ask the vocational expert if there is any other work that the hypothetical person could do that exists in significant numbers in the national economy.

For now, this question needs to be a hypothetical situation because the Judge has not yet made any official findings regarding the claimant's RFC. However, the limitations are not just invented out of thin air. The limitations presented are what the Judge is considering for the RFC in the case. Sometimes, the Judge will pose several hypothetical situations to get the vocational expert's response for each. This is the Judge's opportunity to alter the potential RFC and see how small changes impact the responses from the vocational expert. So just because you hear limitations posed to the vocational expert, that does not mean the RFC has been decided, it hasn't. Most likely, one of those hypothetical scenarios will be the RFC that goes into the decision. If the Judge has already decided on the RFC, the Judge may pose just one hypothetical scenario.

In response to each hypothetical set of limitations, the vocational expert will either say there are no occupations the hypothetical person could do, or will identify specific occupations that could be performed by a person with those limitations. The vocational expert will also say how many specific jobs exist for each occupation throughout the country. For example, the vocational expert might say the person could be a cashier, and that there are over 1,000,000 cashier jobs nationwide. The vocational expert will state the number of jobs so that the Judge can decide if there are a "significant number" of jobs in the national economy.

What is a *significant* number of jobs? SSA regulations do not define this term, so this is up to the Judge. If it's more than a few thousand across the country, most Judges consider that significant. In most circumstances, the vocational expert will identify two or three occupations, and as long as the combined number of jobs is significant, the Judge can use that evidence to deny the claim. However, this is not required. Just one occupation with a significant number of jobs is sufficient to deny a claim. The bottom line is that regardless of how many occupations are identified, as long as there are a significant number of jobs that exist in the national economy that the claimant can do, that claim will be denied.

It's important to note that Step 5 is a nationwide consideration, so that claimants who live in small towns have the same law apply to them as claimants who live in big cities. In other words, it doesn't matter if the occupations identified by the vocational expert exist in your town or not. There may, in fact, be no one hiring at all in your town, but that is not something the Judge will consider. At Step 5, the Judge will only consider whether occupations exist that you can do, and whether, nationally, there are a significant number of jobs within those occupations (not job openings, total jobs, even if they are all filled and no one is hiring).

Since the plumber can do light work, and since there are over 1,000,000 cashier jobs nationwide, our unfortunate plumber will not be receiving disability benefits after all. In Chapter 17, I will explain how the vocational expert knows whether someone with certain limitations can do a specific occupation. I will explain where that information comes from and how it is presented. For now, all you need to know is that the vocational expert exists, and this person's role at the hearing is critical for making a decision at Steps 4 and 5 of the sequential evaluation process. This is the expert witness who will provide the evidence the Judge will rely on for these vocational findings, and there is almost nothing you can do to influence that testimony.

PART 3: Hearing and Appeals

13. Administrative Law Judges

It's best to start the discussion of SSA staff by introducing the person whose name will be on your decision: the Administrative Law Judge (ALJ). I applied to be an ALJ twice. I also wrote decisions for, and worked with, at least two dozen ALJs during my tenure with SSA. While no two ALJs are the same, there is a profile that SSA seems to prefer. As someone who has a lot of sympathy for persons who have a variety of impairments, and as someone who feels that even a 40 hour workweek is often too much for many people, I do not fit that profile. As such, I am not surprised that I was not selected to be an ALJ.

I wanted to include a section in this book explaining how ALJs are hired, but in doing so, I faced two obstacles. First, I needed to sign several non-disclosure agreements promising to never reveal the format, contents, or procedure of the ALJ examination, or SSA would not consider my applications to be an ALJ. Second, the way ALJs are hired changed significantly in 2018. Many of the Judges currently serving were hired under the old system, but SSA is now hiring under the new system as well. As a result, I decided the best thing to do would be to briefly explain both systems to you, revealing what I can without violating any of the non-disclosure agreements.

The old process for hiring was intense, and could take several years, even for successful applicants. It included an application, a timed assessment that could be done from home, another timed assessment that was done in Washington, D.C., and an interview that was done near Washington, D.C. (with the applicant paying all travel expenses). At the end, every applicant who passed was given a score, and veterans received an additional 5 or 10 points. As a result, many of the people that SSA hired to be Judges under the old system have a history of military service, and some continue to serve in the military reserves. The new hiring system is much more streamlined. Not only are there fewer steps, but that costly trip to the nation's capital has been eliminated. That's good, because those travel expenses were previously a barrier that could have kept good applicants from getting all the way through the process.

As I said, the old system, under which most of the Judges currently serving were hired, included a hiring preference for veterans. These are people who served their country, who have worked their entire lives (many since age 18), and who may have little tolerance for someone whose life does not transpire like theirs. I cannot recall how many times a Judge that was or is in the military told me something like, "If I can work, so can he!" referring to the unfortunate claimant who is about to receive an unfavorable decision. This can change, however, as Judges age and deteriorating health takes a toll. Judges are typically hired in their 40s, and most young Judges are relatively healthy. But everyone ages and health issues become common over time.

Not all Judges fit the profile I just described. Some have dealt with a history of chronic medical conditions, either for themselves or one of their family members. Those Judges tend to have more sympathy for claimants who experience medical challenges. And as those other relatively healthy Judges age, so too does their degree of sympathy rise. A knee or back surgery with many months of grueling rehab will do that to a person! I knew a Judge who denied a high percentage of his cases, until he fell and needed to have a serious back surgery. After that, he considered claimant allegations of pain very differently, and he approved more cases than he denied.

But SSA prefers Judges who deny a high percentage of cases. I know this because, once hired, SSA keeps an eye on Judges to make sure they keep denying cases as planned. SSA conducts periodic reviews of its Judges, but not all Judges. While I am sure SSA would disagree with this observation, in my experience, SSA judicial reviews tend to focus on Judges who approve a high percentage of their cases, while Judges who deny more cases receive less scrutiny.

When I worked at the Appeals Council, which is the office at Headquarters that handles appeals within SSA, part of my job was to conduct reviews of hearing offices or Judges that upper management was not happy with. Some of these reviews were due to serious concerns of bias, but often the problem was simply that the office or specific Judge under review was paying too many cases. That's right, *paying too many cases.* I don't remember ever reviewing a Judge who was *denying* too many cases.

In fact, I often found the favorable decisions from the Judges we reviewed to be well supported. We reviewed favorable decisions for cases that had already closed, so we had access to the entire medical record and the Judge's findings. The record almost always contained objective evidence such as x-ray or MRI studies, and the claimant's allegations of pain tended to match the physical examination findings in reports from the claimant's doctors. I felt most of the favorable decisions were well written, and were well supported by the medical evidence. I was happy to see that those claimants were awarded benefits.

But my colleagues constantly disagreed, explaining they would have decided the case differently. ALJs are allowed to decide a case a certain way as long as there is "substantial evidence" to support the decision. Of course, just like for "severe impairment," this phrase also has a definition that does not make much sense. The United States Supreme Court has defined "substantial evidence" as "more than a mere scintilla of evidence" to support the findings in the decision. In other words, the Judge needs to see more than a tiny amount of evidence supporting the decision.

This also means that even if the majority of the evidence perhaps supports a decision the opposite way, that's fine, as long as there is *some* evidence the Judge can rely on, and that some is *more than a mere scintilla*. This standard gives the ALJ a significant amount of discretion when deciding whether someone is disabled. Most cases have enough evidence that could support a decision either way, meaning the Judge could approve or deny the claim and there would be sufficient evidence to justify that decision.

Most favorable decisions that I reviewed met the standard, meaning they were supported by *more than a mere scintilla* of medical evidence. But don't ask a bunch of lawyers to provide an opinion on a set of facts unless you truly want their opinion. At the Appeals Council, we were told that as long as the case was supported by *substantial evidence*, we should leave it alone. But everyone has an opinion, and everyone wants to be the Judge, so leaving decisions alone was very difficult for most of my former attorney colleagues. They wanted to delve into the evidence and make their own decision, and usually that meant making a decision that was different from the one made by the ALJ who actually decided that case. We were reviewing mostly favorable decisions, so finding them to have fault meant determining the decision should not have been favorable. Everything was skewed in the direction of finding error with favorable decisions. I now know that SSA wanted it this way.

I never conducted a review of a Judge who had a high denial rate. SSA likes those Judges, so they weren't likely to be reviewed for extra scrutiny. Part of the reason for this is the existential crisis in which the Appeals Council constantly finds itself. Congress has established in law that every claimant has the right to a hearing with an ALJ. However, Congress did not create the Appeals Council, it was created by SSA to keep appeals in-house. Every so often, someone points out that the hundreds of employees at the Appeals Council are really completely unnecessary, and cost the taxpayer substantial money with little benefit.

If the ALJ denies your case, you can appeal to the Appeals Council, but they deny most of those appeals (I will discuss appeals more in Chapter 20). At that point, your only option is to sue the Commissioner of Social Security in Federal Court. The reason I say there is little benefit to having the Appeals Council is that because they deny most appeals, most unfavorable decisions will end up in Federal Court anyway, so there really is no need for an appeals entity within SSA itself.

This leaves the Appeals Council with a never-ending need to justify its own existence. It does this in two ways. First, it conducts the "focused reviews" of specific Judges and specific hearing offices that I described above. As I said above, these reviews focus on offices and Judges who are *paying too many cases*. These studies are used by SSA to show Congress that too many Judges are paying too much in benefits to claimants who do not deserve them. Everyone hates "fraud, waste, and abuse," and if you want to find those things, you can find them anywhere because these terms have very little actual meaning. I discuss this in Chapter 33.

Also, by conducting in depth reviews that show the deficiencies only in the favorable decisions, this sends a message to the ALJs: Unless you want to be reviewed with the extra scrutiny, stigma, and training that comes along with it, make sure you aren't *paying too many cases*. This, in turn, encourages more unfavorable decisions, which claimants must then appeal to the Appeals Council. Good job security for those Appeals Council employees, isn't it?

The other thing the Appeals Council does to justify its own existence happens once they get all those appeals from claimants. When they feel the need to justify being part of the process, the Appeals Council will send a lot of decisions back to ALJs, whether they are truly deficient or not. Think of it this way. If a plumber fixed a clog, and the person in charge of checking the work had the ability to shove an old rag back into the hole and re-clog it, then is that quality control check really helping, or just causing more problems? If you want to get noticed, and the Appeals Council does, you shove that old rag back into the hole as many times as you can.

I decided to include this information here, in the ALJ Chapter, because this behavior from the Appeals Council directly impacts the decisions the ALJs issue at the hearing level. The ALJs understand how the Appeals Council operates, and they understand that the Appeals Council likes to get noticed. The ALJs are discouraged from *paying too many cases* because they do not want extra scrutiny, but they also know that if they issue too many unfavorable decisions, those will be appealed, and they will end up getting more cases back from the Appeals Council.

The key takeaway from all of this is that the Judges are not the blindfold wearing, neutral arbiters you thought they would be when you began reading this book. Judges are human, and they have opinions, tendencies, biases, and concerns. They are also swayed by incentives. SSA looks at a person's history closely before deciding whether to hire that person as an ALJ. SSA ends up with a lot of

68

Judges who tend to not be very sympathetic to Social Security Disability claimants. Then, after hiring those unsympathetic Judges, SSA strongly encourages those new Judges to deny as many claims as they can justify.

If you have a case going before an ALJ, know that you cannot choose your Judge, and that the Judge has very specific personality traits, life experiences, and incentives that may not be in your favor. Don't let the black robe fool you. Before you ever set foot in the hearing room, or pick up the phone to dial into your phone hearing, the Judge has already reviewed the evidence in your case, and may have already made a decision as well.

If, after a long hearing, the Judge provides just one extended hypothetical set of work related limitations to the vocational expert, and the vocational expert responds with three occupations containing a significant number of jobs in the national economy, that's bad. This means the Judge had already decided the RFC, and held that hearing solely to gather evidence to justify the upcoming unfavorable decision. You never had a chance at being approved. The Judge had decided to issue an unfavorable decision before your hearing even began. Hopefully, you now have a better idea as to why this was the case.

14. Attorneys and Other Staff

Shortly after I began working for SSA, I went to speak with my manager about a case where I felt the Judge had not considered all of the evidence in an appropriate manner. I provided a coherent, logical argument, and I expected the manager would speak with the Judge and resolve the issue in a way that was fair, impartial, and as I expected for a Federal Judge with an annual salary of $180,000. I was wrong.

The answer I received was "Remember, you work for the Judge. If they could write all of their own decisions, they would. But they can't. So, they need you to write their decisions for them. But you write what they want, not what you want." The point my manager was making is that everyone in the office is there to provide support for the Judges. *Everyone*. That is the number one goal and purpose of the rest of the staff. So now let's meet that staff, so you know who else is involved in getting your medical record developed, managing your hearing, and getting your decision written and mailed out to you.

First, obviously, we have the Administrative Law Judges. Their job is to review the evidence before the hearing, hold the hearing, make a decision on the outcome of the case, and draft a page of instructions for writing the actual decision. These instructions are written using SSA shorthand, and the code is then deciphered by the Attorney Advisor decision writers who draft the actual decisions. The Judges *do not* write their own decisions, although they do get the opportunity to edit the decisions after they have been drafted.

After the Judge makes a decision and drafts the shorthand instructions, those instructions are sent to someone like me. I was an

Attorney Advisor decision writer. This position used to be staffed by non-attorneys over a decade ago, but during the time I was there, hundreds of attorneys were hired, and now the job is almost exclusively done by attorneys. The formal job title is "Attorney Advisor," but the Judges and management refer to Attorney Advisors as "decision writers," or, patronizingly, as just "writers."

The attorneys see this as belittling commentary from the managers, most of whom did not go to law school, take the bar exam, or acquire a license to practice law. It is also insulting when the Judges use this term, because while they are also lawyers, not referring to us as "attorneys" shows little respect to the people who earn half as much salary and yet do twice as much work. I cannot tell you how many Judges have told me "I couldn't do the job that you do." Yet, often those Judges will refer to the attorneys in the office as "writers" as though they have no capacity for independent thought or professional legal analysis. I think this is because they want the attorneys to be robots who do as they are told. Remember what my first manager told me. The Attorney Advisor decision writer writes the Judge's decision. In other words, don't ask questions, just write.

But the job is not nearly that simple. The Attorney Advisor decision writers are required to review large records, often with thousands of pages of complicated medical evidence. They have to listen to the audio recording of the hearing. They also need to check SSA regulations, analyze medical evidence, analyze testimony, provide an in depth discussion of every medical opinion in the record, and finalize a complete, comprehensive, persuasive, and legally sufficient decision that can withstand appellate review. Earlier, I told you that I averaged about two cases per workday, which means I spent an average of just four hours per case. It's a lot to do in a short amount of time and it takes great skill.

However, not every case is the same. SSA allows the attorneys to spend more time drafting unfavorable or partially favorable decisions than favorable decisions. The reason is that unfavorable and partially favorable decisions tend to be longer and more complex. They require additional justification so they can withstand appeal, whereas SSA presumes that claimants will not want to appeal favorable decisions. The Attorney Advisors are allotted around 10 hours for unfavorable or partially favorable decisions, but only around four hours for favorable decisions. However, no additional time is allotted for asking questions, assisting colleagues, and speaking with the Judge about the decision. Thus, any time the Attorney Advisor decision writer spends on those aspects of the job is essentially deducted from the time available to review the medical evidence and draft the decision.

I would often find that speaking with the Judge was necessary to ensure an accurate decision. Some Judges are open to discussion, persuasion, and ultimately challenging their initial view on a case. Perhaps they missed a key piece of evidence, which is not unheard of in a medical record of over 1,000 pages. Or perhaps they just needed to hear the evidence interpreted in a different way. Sometimes the Judge does not apply the complicated regulations correctly. They are required to decide a lot of cases each month, so they also have to move quickly, and sometimes they miss things. A Judge who is open to hearing what the attorneys have to say, who respects the valuable experience and analytical abilities of the attorneys, and who allows the attorneys to write the decisions in a way that is consistent with the evidence, is the easiest to write for and therefore to work with.

On the other hand, a Judge who digs in their heels, refuses to listen to counter-arguments, and ultimately has an "I am the Judge,

72

do what I say" attitude is nearly impossible to write for. Often those decisions do not have a logical flow because the decision is not supported by the evidence. Those Judges are often unhappy and send decisions back to the attorneys to be revised. But it's hard to revise such a decision, so all one can do is follow the Judge's commands, and move it along, knowing it will probably be sent back on appeal. In such a circumstance, it becomes clear that the ability to skillfully and intentionally misinterpret medical evidence and claimant testimony is an unofficial job requirement for the Attorney Advisor decision writer position.

The office also has staff who gather the evidence, call claimants to schedule hearings, manage communication with representatives, and handle all of the other legwork that is required to open the case, complete the medical record, and make sure everything goes smoothly for the Judges and attorneys. These staff members are called Case Technicians, and I will not pretend to know how they do their jobs. I know from observation they work extremely hard, and at $40,000 to $50,000 per year, the taxpayer is getting a real bargain.

Above the attorneys and the front office staff, but *not* the Judges, is the management team. Some managers seem like they are constantly busy, and for others, I legitimately cannot figure out what they do all day long. Some managers know the SSA disability system extremely well, and others could not name the five steps of the sequential evaluation process. They all get paid around $110,000 to $130,000 per year, regardless of program knowledge or level of effort. They provide performance evaluation for all staff, including the attorneys, at the end of each fiscal year (the government schedule operates on a *fiscal year*, which runs from October 1st to September 30th). The attorneys get annoyed when a non-attorney manager, who does not know the ins and outs of the Attorney Advisor job, completes their performance evaluations.

The management team in a hearing office consists of the Hearing Office Director (HOD), who is in charge of everyone except for the Judges. Right below the Hearing Office Director are the Group Supervisors, who each supervise a group of case technicians and attorneys. The Hearing Office Director and the Group Supervisors are often not attorneys, yet this management team supervises an office in one of the largest adjudicatory systems in the world. I was once told that if the Social Security Disability adjudicatory machine was its own country, it would be within the top 10 largest worldwide by volume of cases filed and decided.

The fact that the management team consists of both attorneys and non-attorneys often leads to friction. Law school teaches you how to think, how to analyze, how to research, how to interpret, and ultimately how to provide arguments and counter-arguments to best understand both sides of an issue. This is something the attorneys and Judges do really well together when they want to. But it also means that a manager who does not have that skill set can sometimes get in the way of the attorneys and Judges doing their jobs.

The management team is itself under a microscope from one of the 10 Regional Offices around the country and from SSA Headquarters. It would certainly be easier for all of the attorneys who keep the legal cogs turning if the entire management team were lawyers, rather than middle managers with their own concerns. Rather than focusing on high quality legal analysis, the managers tend to worry about finishing cases, achieving production goals, impressing their bosses, and ultimately self-preservation. Like most private sector middle managers, they want to look good so they can keep their jobs and so they can move up within the organization.

74

These mismatched incentives cause a great deal of friction. The non-attorney managers who have never done the Attorney Advisor decision writer job simply do not understand it. They do not understand the skill set of attorneys, or the pressure of drafting a persuasive decision within a strict time limit. There is no way to fully understand this job short of doing it for at least a year. The best non-attorney managers, and there are some excellent ones, are those who listen to their team members, and provide assistance to help them get their work done. The worst managers, regardless of whether they are attorneys, are the ones who engage in one-way communication: I talk *at* you, you listen *to* me, and you go do your work without complaining. That situation does not work for long. Productivity lags, and eventually employees who do not feel heard or appreciated decide it's time to leave.

But this is not even the worst case scenario. That occurs when a manager takes credit for the accomplishments of the employees being supervised, while passing blame down to those employees if production slows. It's even worse when the manager's action or inaction is the direct cause of lagging production. Yet, many managers will blame the employees being supervised so the manager can avoid getting into trouble with upper management.

Here is an example of this situation. I once wrote decisions for a Judge who was incredibly slow and simply could not handle the size of her caseload. Judges are required to issue a certain number of decisions each month. But this Judge was slow, so for any case she could not complete by the end of the month, she would return that case to the Attorney Advisor decision writer, blaming the attorney for not following her decision instructions.

That is a strong and serious allegation, and it's not something that management takes lightly. When I reported the situation to my

Group Supervisor, he brought it to the Hearing Office Director. But that person did not want to upset the Judge. No one ever wants to upset the Judge. So, the managers reported to the Regional Office that the Judge was right and it was the Attorney Advisor decision writers who were to blame. We were accused of not doing our jobs correctly, even though several Attorney Advisor decision writers were involved, and yet the common denominator in that situation was the Judge.

It was clear who was at fault. It was clear she could not handle her caseload. But the situation was allowed to continue. Still, the Judge could not play this game forever, and she was eventually pressured to step down. I don't know what was worse about that situation, the Judge throwing under the bus the Attorney Advisor decision writers that she relied on to draft her decisions, or the fact that when this situation was presented to management, they did the same thing to avoid upsetting the Judge.

This is not the only way that managers sabotage the careers of those they are supposed to supervise and mentor. Often, the Attorney Advisor decision writers will apply for other jobs within SSA. A good manager will want to support their team members and help them with well-deserved career advancement. In contrast, a bad manager who only cares about self-preservation will act differently. If management does not want to lose a highly productive Attorney Advisor decision writer, the manager will give that person a bad reference so the person cannot move on to a different role. This happened to me, as well as to several of my colleagues. For me, that was the last straw. When I discovered through a friend's Freedom of Information Act (FOIA) request that my manager had sabotaged my application for a different position, I decided advancement was never going to happen, and it was time to leave SSA.

76

Now that I have introduced the office staff, I think it's only fair that you know and understand how the Attorney Advisor decision writer that will be drafting the decision in your case is evaluated by management. This way, you can understand the incentive structure this person works under and thinks about when they are drafting your decision. A lot of people think that government workers are lazy, that they spend a lot of their day just standing around chatting, and that they frankly don't work much. "Good enough for government work" is a saying that suggests that anyone who chooses a career in public service does so because they are not competent to work in the private sector.

That could not be further from the truth. Many people leave law school with well over $100,000 of student loan debt, and therefore cannot afford to enter into public service. They need the hours, the overtime, and clients with deep pockets to pay off their enormous debt. But I planned ahead, and I left law school with a manageable amount of debt, which allowed me to accept a public service position. I wanted a job where I would work 40 hours per week, with overtime only if I felt like it. I wanted a job where I would be serving hardworking taxpayers, to make their lives a little bit better. In other words, for me, and for many other Social Security employees, public service was a deliberate decision.

The colleagues I worked with over the years at Social Security had different reasons for working there, but the ones who stayed had the same public service goals that I had. Everyone wants to be paid fairly, but public servants understand that their positions are taxpayer-funded, and they want the taxpayer to get the most bang for their buck.

To ensure this, SSA has worked with Congress to establish production metrics to ensure that its employees are utilizing their 40 hours per week in a productive manner. Judges and other support staff have their own goals and metrics, and I am not in a position to discuss those because I do not have sufficient knowledge to do so accurately. But as I have said, it's the Attorney Advisor decision writer who will be drafting the decision, and I think it's fair for you to know what that person faces on a daily basis regarding production standards. This is something the attorneys think about *constantly*. It will be something the attorney will be thinking about while drafting *your* decision.

When I worked for SSA, there were four categories under which the Attorney Advisor decision writers were evaluated: participation, job knowledge, achieves business results, and interacting with others. At the end of the year, the person is given one of three possible ratings for each category: a "1" indicates unsatisfactory performance; a "3" indicates satisfactory performance; and a "5" indicates outstanding performance. The Attorney Advisor is given a rating in each category during the official performance evaluation at the end of the U.S. government's fiscal year. A "1" is rare, you really have to seriously screw something up to get a "1." Most people get a "3" in most categories. What every employee wants to know, and strives for all year long, is how a rating of "5" can be achieved. The reason is that, of the four scores being assigned, an employee needs at least two "5" ratings to receive a performance-based award, which often comes with a modest monetary bonus.

Let's now look at what each category means. I want you to fully understand the motivation that the Attorney Advisor decision writer has at the time your decision is being drafted. The category of "participation" is fairly nebulous. When we had meetings or trainings, I noticed that raising one's hand and asking questions is

78

useful for achieving a "3" or a "5" in this category, but there isn't much else to say because it's just not a category that applies much to a person who sits alone at a desk and writes most of the day.

Similarly, "interacting with others" is often difficult to do in such an isolated position. As long as one shows respect to management, and communicates diligently with Judges, a "3" is almost assured. When we did work in an actual office before the pandemic, I had an open door policy for fellow attorneys, who could drop in and talk to me about a case anytime. I was a "go to" person for all kinds of questions, and I took pride in that. Sometimes I received a "3" in this category, and sometimes I received a "5." These two categories are so vague that management could assign either score, but like I said, they would not assign a "1" unless something went seriously wrong.

The area of "job knowledge" is a bit more measurable, but it takes time to really understand how deep a person's job knowledge is. The Social Security regulations are quite complex, and as I said, it takes over a year to develop a deep knowledge base. I was really interested in the details of the regulations, so other attorneys, and even Judges, would often come to me with technical questions. Once management understood that I was a valuable resource to the office, I never received anything below a "5" in this category. Although, I do recognize it is difficult to acquire deep job knowledge when you feel like you never have enough time to do so, because you are always trying to finish that next decision.

The final area of consideration is "achieves business results." This is really the only one of the four categories that is constantly, and I do mean on a daily basis, reiterated by management. This is also, unsurprisingly, the most objective category. This is where the idea of the lazy public servant will disappear. Earlier, I explained that the attorneys have only a certain amount of time to review the medical record, listen to the hearing recording, draft the decision, ask questions, assist colleagues, and speak with the Judge about the decision. I referenced 10 hours for an unfavorable decision and four hours for a favorable decision. This is where those timeframes originate.

The way this category works is that someone who does not do this job decided it takes a certain amount of time to do it. A favorable decision takes X many hours, and an unfavorable decision takes Y many hours. So, the attorneys are measured against these completely arbitrary metrics, regardless of the size of the medical record, how long the hearing is, how many medical opinions there are, how extensive the discussion with the Judge needs to be, etc.

Here is how it works. The credit given for drafting an unfavorable decision is around 10 hours. If, during a 40 hour week, an attorney does four of those, 40 hours of credit would be given. Because this was achieved in 40 hours of time, the production rate is 100%. If the attorney did five decisions, 50 hours of credit earned divided by 40 hours would mean the production rate would be 125%. With only three decisions drafted, 30 hours of credit earned divided by 40 hours would mean the production rate would be just 75%. As I said previously, SSA assumes favorable decisions can be a lot shorter since there is little chance of them being appealed, so for those cases only four hours of credit is given.

Like the Judges, the attorneys are assessed on a monthly basis. So, at the end of a month, if there were four work weeks totaling 160 work hours, the person would need to have earned 160 hours of credit to maintain a 100% production rate. Too low, and the person receives a "1" in this category at the annual performance evaluation. But if it's high enough, the person receives a "5." Even

80

though the final production rate is not calculated until the end of the fiscal year, this is something the attorneys are constantly thinking about. No one ever wants to fall behind, because if you do, it is unbelievably difficult to catch up.

While members of Congress might like this type of objective measurement system because they see it as holding employees accountable, in fact all it does is cause highly-educated attorneys to set their knowledge, skill, and ability aside, and prioritize speed above all else. But prioritizing speed leads to all the problems you would expect. The most obvious issue is that the decisions tend to be incomplete. Medical opinions are often missed, there tends to be a lot of unsupported conclusions, and sometimes highly relevant evidence is not discussed. The result is more cases being sent back to the ALJ on appeal, which is known as a "remand."

To avoid such problems, the quality of the decision needs to be considered alongside speed. When both factors are considered equally, that is called *efficiency*. You can see, then, that when one only focuses on speed, the taxpayer loses out. Far more time is then spent on the case as it goes to the Appeals Council, then comes back to the hearing level for a new hearing and a new decision. This would be unnecessary if it were done right the first time.

Paraphrasing a quote by American basketball coach John Wooden, "If you don't have the time to do it right, you don't have the time to do it again." I would constantly think about this quote throughout my agency career. SSA says it tries to be very efficient, but it is, in reality, highly inefficient. Everyone is pushed to move so quickly that many decisions contain unnecessary errors, forcing SSA to take time to "do it again." Further, the absurd production standards cause so much frustration that many people just decide to leave. Then, SSA needs to hire and train new staff, a process that takes well over a year to complete. More inefficiency.

If SSA just scrapped these metrics, or made them more realistic, they would have happier, more productive attorney employees who feel they are being treated like legal professionals. There would be less stress, less turnover, less need to train new employees, and fewer remanded cases. To me, that's real efficiency. To me, that would give the taxpayer real value.

Unfortunately, the problems do not end with simply having an inefficient agency. Do you remember when I said the credit given to the attorneys for an unfavorable decision is the same 10 hours no matter how much evidence is in the record? Did you think about who assigns the cases to the Attorney Advisor decision writers? The managers do that, the Hearing Office Director and the Group Supervisors. This allows the managers to support or sabotage the careers of the employees that they supervise.

Any manager with power can make or break an employee's career. This is certainly true for the managers within SSA. If the management team wants to help a particular employee, or make themselves look good, they can assign the person cases that have less evidence. For those cases, it will take less time to draft the decision. But the reverse is also true. It takes way more time to draft a decision if the case has a large medical record and/or a lot of medical opinions. The 10 hours of credit anticipates that an attorney will be given some cases with smaller medical records and some with larger medical records. The metric assumes that an attorney will be given some cases with one or two medical opinions and some cases with six or seven. In other words, the case credit is supposed to represent the average number of hours it takes to draft an average case. Throughout the year, all of the attorneys should receive a mix of cases, so that one metric can be used to assess everyone in the same way.

But what if this initial premise is not true? Let's say the average unfavorable decision has a 700 page medical record. I am making that number up, using it for a relative comparison here, but in my office this was close to accurate. If you give someone cases that all have 300-400 pages of medical evidence, that person might have a production rate well over 100%. Conversely, if you consistently give the person cases that all have 2,000 pages of medical evidence, there is no way that person will ever be a successful employee, no matter how good they are at their job.

I saw management do this to someone they clearly wanted to get rid of. We called it "stacking." Management would "stack" the employee with one 2,000 page record after another. Today almost all SSA disability cases have electronic records. However, a few paper cases do still linger within SSA. There used to be more of those, and sometimes you would see a stack of thick manilla folders placed one on top of the other on the person's desk. This is where the term comes from. If management wanted you out, and if they stacked one huge medical record on top of another, there was almost nothing you could do about it except quit. Once those cases start, there is simply no way out from under the deluge.

If you ask SSA management, I have no doubt they would deny that this ever happens. But I saw it happen to a colleague of mine, and I can tell you that it does. The SSA case management system keeps a record of every case and the Attorney Advisor decision writer assigned to draft that decision. All one would have to do is look up my employee friend, check the cases the employee was assigned during the year before leaving SSA, and check the sizes of all of those medical records. There is evidence of stacking, if you know where to look for it.

But why would a manager want someone out, especially if the person is a productive employee? Middle managers are given directives from above. In the case of Social Security Disability, this means the 10 Regional Offices around the country and SSA Headquarters. The top offices need to have middle managers below them who will listen, obey directives, and keep control of their employees. Those middle managers, in turn, need to have employees under them who will be similarly obedient without questioning why a particular policy exists. They need people who will do what they are told, won't complain, won't assert any of their union rights, won't file union grievances, and who in the end won't stir up any trouble by suggesting that any other employee do any of these things.

Non-manager SSA employees work in positions that are governed by contracts with the National Treasury Employees Union (NTEU) or the American Federation of Government Employees (AFGE). Even employees who choose not to join these two unions still fall under many of their protections. But government managers, just as in the private sector, will do whatever they can to limit employees from exercising their union rights. In the eyes of management, the best employees are the ones who put their heads down, don't question authority, and do what they are told, even when the directive is some ridiculous policy that negatively impacts employees or runs contrary to public service.

The power to ruin a career also goes the other way. Management can use their ability to selectively assign cases to make themselves or their group look really good. In other words, they can also bolster the careers of their subordinates, when they want to.

84

Cases are supposed to be assigned "first in, first out." This means that when an attorney needs a new case, that person should be assigned whatever the next oldest case is, regardless of the size of the medical record or how many medical opinions are in the record. This would result in the same average case size for each employee. That is how SSA would tell you it assigns cases, but that was not how things actually transpired when I was there.

The Group Supervisors also have performance evaluations. They want to have productive employees because that makes them look good. In my group, for much of the time I was with that office, we had an ethical Group Supervisor who followed the rules. As a result, I was assigned a mix of cases. However, I would often notice a lot of cases in a row with larger medical records, and other people in my group would notice the same thing. We had an inclination as to what was happening, but no solid proof. I was later able to find proof, but I could not bring that proof out of the office because it included protected information, such as Social Security numbers. But I no longer work for SSA, so I can now divulge that this occurred.

While my Group Supervisor was ethical and would assign the cases in order, another group had an unethical Group Supervisor who would go into the queue of cases waiting to be drafted, check the size of the medical record, and assign that person's own group cases with the smallest records. Of course, with fewer pages of medical evidence to review, those attorneys were able to draft cases faster, which made that group and its attorneys seem more productive.

In contrast, my group would often find that we had been assigned several cases in a row with large medical records. This means that in my group, the average medical record was significantly higher than it was for the other group. All of the attorneys were paid the same, but the attorneys in my group had to review more pages of medical evidence. We also had to write longer decisions. When there is more evidence, there is more evidence to evaluate, and thus the decisions are longer. We were all paid the same but some of us had to do more work because we ended up in the wrong group. All so a corrupt middle manager could take credit for other people's work, without caring how those actions impacted other employees.

Managers have the power to create a struggling employee by stacking cases and inundating them with large medical records. However, managers also have the ability to help struggling employees by giving them cases with small medical records that will take less time to review, which of course means less time is needed to draft the decision. Using the prior example, if an attorney has a mix of cases with an average medical record of around 700 pages and still struggles, management could overwhelm that person such that they underperform, and then quit or get fired. But they could also do the opposite of stacking, assigning that employee several cases in a row with smaller medical records so that person never drops into the "1" range of unsatisfactory performance. A manager may also have a selfish reason for doing this. The manager may want to avoid questions from the Regional Office or Headquarters about the struggling employee, so they may try to help the employee in order to remove the spotlight from their group. I saw this happen too.

As I said earlier, for those employees they don't like, managers can assign difficult cases. They could also manipulate the performance evaluations of those employees, but this is too risky. It would be weird if someone who had a reputation of being the "go to" person in the office started getting "1s" on the annual

86

performance evaluations. Everything in the federal government leaves a paper trail, and no manager wants to be caught doing something unethical. Giving someone "1s" is just too flashy, it attracts attention.

Instead, if management does not like a person who is clearly producing well, and who is an objective high-value asset to the office, they can simply give the person "3s" in all four categories and leave them alone. With no "5s" that person will not get a performance-based award, and that's not fair if the employee deserves one because of their hard work and dedication to public service. And again, if management *really* wants someone out, instead of giving "1s" on the annual performance evaluation, management can instead assign the person cases with enormous medical records, drown them in medical evidence over a period of many months, let them fall behind, and over the course of a year or two, gradually push them out. This is, admittedly, a rare circumstance, but it happens.

It is possible for someone to fight back and to demand an investigation, but many employees never get that far. For many people, it's just easier to decide not to stay somewhere they are clearly undervalued and underutilized. The unions like to see employees push back and fight for their rights, but that often is not what the employee wants in such a situation.

At this point you may have several thoughts. Can't anything be done to stop this manipulation? Aren't the taxpaying claimants supposed to be the number one priority for the Social Security Administration? Who supervises the Group Supervisors and the Hearing Office Director anyway? There is one more staff member that I have not yet introduced. An office can have as little as one or two Judges, or it can have a couple dozen. But every office does have someone who is untimely in charge.

The Hearing Office Chief Administrative Law Judge (HOCALJ) is above everyone, including the management team. This is the person who would, theoretically, make sure that no one is abusing their authority or manipulating the system to unfairly advantage some employees over others. But this Judge also holds hearings, makes decisions, edits decision drafts, and has to attend endless conference call meetings with the Regional Office and Headquarters. As a result, in practice, this Judge is too busy to exercise any real degree of supervision over the office's management team. This allows the managers to have free reign, virtually unsupervised, to treat the rest of the staff however they see fit.

The number one goal for the managers is always the same, and it is not good customer service or a fair process for the claimants. The management team's sole focus, at all times, is on closing however many cases Headquarters has listed for that month's goal. This makes them look good and helps them with career advancement. It also helps the managers to receive good scores on their own performance evaluations.

It is for this reason that managers will cheat, blame their staff when things go wrong, and take credit for success when things go well. As long as the office hits it's assigned goal, that's all that counts. If the office reaches its goal, the HOCALJ is happy, even if in achieving this goal, the staff have been mistreated, statistics have been manipulated, taxpaying claimants have been ignored, and good employees have been driven out.

While you are sitting at home hoping the professional staff at the Social Security Administration are carefully considering the

88

evidence in your case, these are the games that are being played by adults behind closed doors. It's wrong, and it's bad customer service. Cases should be assigned randomly, by a computer that does not have human prejudices, taking into account the size of the medical record for each case. Managers should not have the power to destroy someone's career, or to manipulate case assignments to boost their own. Until SSA changes how cases are assigned, all the performance metrics do is cause unnecessary stress. They don't actually measure anything except perhaps how ethical a particular manager is. They certainly do not achieve better decisions, more efficiency, happier workers, or excellence in public service.

When you get your decision, and you are reading it, thinking, "How could the Judge have written *that*?" or "Wait, that's not my *entire* statement!" or perhaps "Hang on, they missed *a lot!*" Now you know that the person writing your decision was not the Judge, but an attorney who is underutilized, who may be working under a manipulative manager, and who is forced to focus solely on speed, speed, speed! Making sure all of the medical evidence was thoroughly considered, making sure your entire testimony was heard, making sure the decision was carefully written, well, those things are simply not prioritized.

15. The Timeline of a Typical Case

Earlier, I described what happens from the time the claimant files the application until the time the claimant files a request for a hearing with an Administrative Law Judge. I explained generally how the initial and reconsideration levels progress through the state agency. Now, I will explain step-by-step how the hearing level unfolds, which will also explain why it takes so darn long!

When an appeal, called a "Request for Hearing with an Administrative Law Judge" is filed, the case sits in a giant virtual national queue with tens of thousands of other cases until someone from the governing hearing office pulls the case into the queue for that office. There are some offices that handle cases from all around the country, but for now let's presume this is a local hearing office with a physical presence in that community. For example, if the claimant lives in San Francisco, California, there is an actual hearing office in that city. Before the pandemic, the person could walk into that office and ask for a CD to be made with the entire case record, and the person could then attend a hearing in person in front of a Judge who lives in that community.

There are a couple hundred such offices all around the country. Beginning in March 2020, all staff were sent home and told to work virtually, although a small skeleton staff still needed to come into the office to check the mail, check the fax machines (yes, SSA still uses those), and keep the computer servers up and running. But because almost everything is done electronically through a massive national case management system, most staff could work from home throughout the pandemic. I began working from home in early March 2020, and I did not return to the office again prior to leaving SSA in July 2021.

90

Once the case has been created, the claimant will provide a list of all doctors, tests, anything known to the claimant regarding medical sources. The case technicians at the hearing office then take over and get as many medical records as they can. Do you remember earlier when I said these staff members are not paid nearly enough for what they do? Have you ever tried to get *your own* medical records from an American medical office? It's a nightmare that takes forever, and they often want to hand you a stack of printed paper and charge you a massive amount for it, even well into the 21st century. The case technicians handle so much of the legwork necessary to develop the medical record, and it really is a thankless job.

Luckily, many claimants at this stage also have a representative who can help develop the medical record and submit what evidence they are able to obtain. But it is also SSA's responsibility to do this, regardless of whether someone has a representative. If a claimant, represented or not, tells SSA there are records with a certain doctor, hospital, or facility, or simply indicates "the VA" as a treatment provider, Social Security must contact the listed source and get whatever records it can. This often results in hundreds or even thousands of pages of evidence, including (especially from the VA), a large amount of duplicate information.

When a person tells SSA they went to a particular hospital or had treatment within a specific healthcare system, that system will send every record it has, even for all kinds of treatment that are irrelevant to the reason the person claims disability. For example, if the person has a back condition (the most common impairment for Social Security Disability claims), SSA does not need all of the claimant's primary care bloodwork, but will inevitably get it anyway. It takes a lot of skill and experience to know what is relevant to a case and what to quickly read past. The Judges and attorneys receive a lot of training in this area.

It takes months to adequately develop the medical record so the Judge knows what questions to ask at the hearing, and so the Attorney Advisor decision writer has evidence to analyze in the written decision. But that's okay, because you will definitely have to wait many months for your hearing anyway. It was not long ago that the average claimant was waiting almost two years for a one hour hearing. Now, the waiting time is under a year, but this still gives the representative and SSA staff plenty of time to gather all of the relevant medical information. This process is, after all, a review of the claimant's medical impairments, so it's very important that the medical record be as complete as possible.

Once all of the expected medical records have arrived, it's time to schedule the hearing, which will be approximately two to four months in the future. A hearing notice is mailed to the claimant and representative indicating the date and time of the hearing, and also the name of the Judge. Judges usually leave around 60 to 90 minutes on their schedule for each hearing.

Before the pandemic, the typical claimant would go in person to a hearing office and sit in front of an ALJ in a small hearing room that contained a raised bench for the Judge, a table for the claimant and representative, the Social Security seal on the wall, and, of course, an American flag. Some claimants would go to a hearing office and appear in front of a Judge on the other side of the country using SSA's internal closed circuit video link technology. Still others would choose to stay home and do a telephone hearing. Beginning in March 2020, all of the hearings were switched to be telephone hearings as the Judges were told they also had to work from home. When I departed SSA, most hearings were still conducted over the phone, although SSA was starting to allow claimants to attend video hearings from home using Microsoft Teams.

In the future, it is likely that many claimants and representatives will continue to prefer to do the hearing from home, or from the representative's office. While SSA does provide transportation reimbursement for claimants who travel to a hearing office, that trek is often difficult for someone with agoraphobia, anxiety, depression, and/or pain. It could also be difficult for someone who needs to use a walker, cane, or wheelchair to travel long distances, particularly in a northern climate. Attending the hearing from home or from the representative's office provides a certain level of comfort and familiarity of surroundings. Such a setting can help to reduce anxiety and improve the degree of information provided in the claimant's testimony. For this reason, I suspect many claimants will continue to choose this method.

As the hearing approaches, if the claimant has a representative, the representative's office will likely be preparing any final evidence submissions and will send them to the hearing office responsible for the case. There is a rule that all evidence has to be submitted one week prior to the hearing so the Judge has time to review it before the hearing. This is a helpful and practical rule that started in the Northeastern United States, and has since been adopted nationwide.

In the past, representatives could bring evidence to the Judge at, literally, the last minute. Sometimes a representative would walk into the hearing room with a stack of new evidence, seconds before the hearing was to begin. Of course, this means the Judge would not have seen this evidence, and would not be familiar with it, so the Judge would not be able to ask the claimant about any of those doctor visits, tests, or procedures. Even though they are supposed to then review that evidence after the hearing, many Judges would not, particularly if there was a lot of new evidence to review.

It is daunting to try and conduct a disability hearing when several hundred pages of disorganized medical evidence show up suddenly just as the hearing is supposed to begin. How might this change the approach the Judge takes to the hearing? What questions might the Judge need to ask that they will not know to ask until after the hearing has concluded? Not having the evidence prior to the hearing often meant that the hearing would need to be done a second time, which is a huge waste of resources. The one week rule is excellent for preventing such a frustrating situation.

For those claimants without a representative, the one week rule also applies, but Judges tend to be less strict when the claimant is not represented. Some Judges may choose to consider the evidence, but they are not required to. Therefore, it's best to have all relevant evidence submitted on time to give yourself the best chance at success.

16. The Hearing

Whether you are appearing in person, on a computer video call, or on a telephone, no doubt you will be nervous when your hearing begins. You have been waiting for this for a very long time, likely well over a year. You don't know exactly what to expect. Even after reading this book, you will still likely be very nervous, which is understandable.

If you need to travel to an SSA hearing office for your hearing, SSA will pay for transportation. This is very helpful since many disability applicants have minimal income and few resources. You should leave plenty of time and plan to arrive early, especially if you will be subject to the whims of bad weather or public transportation schedules.

Whether you arrive in person at the hearing office, or virtually via the computer or telephone, the hearing commences and proceeds basically the same way each time. The Judge, likely wearing a black robe, will suddenly start talking, "We are now on the record. Are you John Doe?" The claimant then answers yes, after which the Judge continues speaking. "Good morning Mr. Doe, my name is Bob Smith and I am an Administrative Law Judge with the Social Security Administration Office of Hearing Operations. I am the Judge who has been assigned to hear your case." If you have a representative, this is where the Judge would confirm the representative's name. The Judge would also ask basic introductory questions about the contact information for both the claimant and the representative, such as mailing address, since decisions are sent by mail.

If you are on your own, you will need to listen carefully and answer all of these questions yourself. You will not be talking about your disability at this point. You would simply follow what the Judge is saying and asking, and respond directly and only to the questions asked. If you have anxiety or another mental health impairment that prevents concentration, well, this is even more of a reason to have a representative handling all of this for you at the hearing. The Judge will ask you about these impairments, but not yet. At this point, there is a lot of information that the Judge is required to gather, and they will not appreciate you slowing them down, even if it's not on purpose. The Judge conducts around 50 hearings per month, or around 12 every week. They need to keep things moving!

The next thing the Judge will do is introduce everyone involved in the hearing. If you are sitting in a hearing room, some of these people may also be sitting in the room with you, but some may be calling into the hearing on the telephone. If you are doing a phone hearing, most likely everyone will be calling in. The Judge needs to say everyone's name for a very specific reason. The hearing, no matter how you and everyone else are attending, is being recorded, but it is an audio recording only. There is no video.

SSA records the audio of all hearings so the Judge, the attorney writing the decision, and anyone reviewing the hearing during an appeal can listen in and make sure the proper procedures were followed. For this reason, the Judge will say things that might seem obvious, such as "I have with me today the claimant, John Doe." The reason things need to be said out loud is the same reason that a radio commentator doing a football game tells you which way each team is moving. A future listener cannot see what is happening. Therefore, anything visible needs to be said out loud to "paint the picture" so that a future listener, such as the Appeals Council, can understand everything that is happening at the hearing.

Next, let's talk about who will be at the hearing. There may be a lot more people there than you would expect. First, we have the Judge. Second, you, the claimant. Assuming you have a representative, that is the third person who will attend the hearing. If you have a witness, such as a friend, family member, colleague, boss, etc., who can attest to your medical conditions, or how they affect your ability to work, those people would also need to be there in person or on call and ready to testify by telephone. The Judge will call anyone you request to testify at your hearing so long as the testimony is relevant to your medical conditions or your ability to work. Finally, there will be at least one, and maybe two or three, other people you have never met attending this hearing.

One person who will be at almost every hearing is the vocational expert. You learned about this person earlier, but you will not meet the vocational expert for your hearing until the hearing begins. As I have said, the vocational expert is an expert on jobs and the economy. This person usually has a master's degree or possibly even a Ph.D. The vocational expert likely worked as a job placement coordinator, helping people find jobs. Something that is difficult for most claimants to understand is that this person is *not* at the hearing to talk about you specifically. I introduced this concept earlier when I discussed the Judge presenting hypothetical scenarios to the vocational expert. The vocational expert is there to listen to these hypothetical scenarios and say whether those hypothetical people could do your past relevant work or other work that exists in significant numbers in the national economy. This person usually testifies at the end of the hearing, so I will return to this person in Chapter 17.

There may be one or two other people attending the hearing, either because your representative requested the attendance of these people, or because the Judge decided their testimony is needed. These people are called medical experts. They are either medical doctors or psychologists. If the issue the Judge needs to know about relates to a physical impairment, the Judge will call a medical doctor. If the issue is a mental health or psychological impairment, the Judge will call a psychiatrist or a psychologist. You can see the resume of the medical expert in the record before or after the case, in case you want to know where they went to school, where they have worked, what specific degree they have attained, etc. The Judge needs to have this information in the record in order to find the person to be a qualified expert. So, if you are curious, if you want to know more about the person behind the voice on the phone during the hearing, you can check for that information in the record.

The person or persons who testify will do so at the request of SSA or your representative, but either way SSA will pay for their services. The claimant will not need to pay anything. The doctor(s) who testify are paid for their time, not based on what they say. In other words, SSA is paying the doctor(s) to analyze the evidence, but not to support a favorable or unfavorable decision. And unlike the vocational expert, this person is at the hearing to review and analyze your medical records and to talk about you. So, who is this doctor that appears out of nowhere to discuss your medical history without ever having met you?

The medical experts who testify can have a variety of backgrounds. As is the case with the state agency medical consultants, many times these are older, retired doctors, who know this process very well. Many of them work as independent contractors, but essentially for one client, Social Security. And many of them do *a lot* of hearings. They know the procedures, they know the Judges, and they know whether a particular Judge likes to approve or deny cases. While they will not be discussing your case with the Judge ahead of time, you have to remember these experts are human, and they want to earn their flat fee in the shortest amount of time. They also want to keep the Judges happy so they continue to be called back in future cases.

This means that if the Judge is someone who denies a lot of cases, the medical expert might...*MIGHT*...take this into account when providing testimony. There is, of course, no way to prove this. I acknowledge it's pure speculation. Still, during my time at SSA, I noticed that the Judges who had high denial rates tended to get opinions from medical experts supporting denials, and the Judges with high approval rates tended to get opinions supporting approvals. Keep this in mind when the Judge tells you this expert witness is a neutral witness who does not work for SSA and who is not being paid to provide specific testimony.

The Judge will call an expert, determine the person to be a qualified expert, and then decide how to evaluate the expert's opinions based on what the expert says and how the Judge wants to decide the case. You may even experience a situation where the Judge wants to deny a claim, calls a particular expert thinking that doctor will provide testimony that could be used to deny the claim, and is then surprised when the expert provides testimony suggesting your impairments are quite disabling. The Judge can accept that testimony and find you disabled, or the Judge can find those opinions unpersuasive, even though the Judge is the one who called the expert to begin with.

As I said before, these experts are paid for their time to review the evidence before the hearing and to testify during the hearing. No one really knows what the expert will say until they speak. Also, no one knows what the Judge will do with that testimony after the hearing. An expert might suggest your impairments are not severe enough to keep you from working, and yet the Judge might still find you disabled. You just never know. Finally, keep in mind that most cases do not involve a medical expert. But since some do, it's important that you are familiar with these witnesses, so you can feel prepared.

Once the Judge gets through all of the introductions, the Judge will go over the evidence in the record and make sure the record is complete. If you or your representative have new evidence, you will need to explain why it was not submitted at least one week prior to the hearing. For example, if you asked for the evidence three months prior to the hearing and you received it the day prior to the hearing, that is a good reason for the Judge to excuse the late submission and allow the evidence. Judges understand that this sometimes happens.

Or, let's say you received the evidence two weeks before the hearing, and then you were in a car accident and in the hospital until the day before the hearing, so you could not submit the evidence one week in advance. That would be another good reason for the late submission. But other excuses, such as "Sorry, I forgot, I have a bad memory" will not be tolerated. If you want the Judge to consider the evidence, you need to get it into the record as soon as you can. If you are not represented, the hearing office will tell you how to submit evidence, and you will need to make sure you do so at least seven days before the hearing.

After the introductory statements, the Judge will administer an oath to everyone who will testify. Your representative does not provide factual evidence. The representative will make a legal argument, which is not testimony, so the representative will not be sworn in. However, the claimant and any witnesses will have to

100

swear/affirm to tell the truth, just like on television. It's a real thing and it's very serious. Remember, the hearing is recorded, and everything that is said by any witness is recorded. All testimony is given under penalty of perjury, and because the hearing is a federal procedure, federal perjury law applies. In other words, *don't lie* unless you want to spend time in federal prison.

If there is a medical expert, or two, that person or persons will usually testify at the beginning of the hearing. It is possible the Judge may ask the claimant questions about the alleged impairments and allow the expert to listen before testifying. However, the medical experts are usually busy people who are only interpreting the written medical records, which they have reviewed prior to the hearing. So, the Judge will usually just start with the medical expert's testimony. The Judge might ask an open-ended question like "Tell me what impairments you see" or may get very specific, such as "Tell me the specific physical activities a person could do after undergoing a back surgery like the one the claimant had done." It all depends on the impairments, the evidence, and the Judge's style.

When the Judge is done asking the medical expert questions, your representative will have a turn. If you do not have a representative, the Judge will ask you if you have any questions for the expert. This is yet another reason why you should have a representative, and it's another example of how they earn their fee. For an unrepresented claimant, it's best to not ask any questions to the medical expert. The Judge has to give you the opportunity because it is required by law. You have a "due process" right to ask questions. But unrepresented claimants do not have the legal education, training, or background to know what to ask or how to ask it. The Judge is required to give you this opportunity, but if you delay the proceedings by asking things that are not within the scope of the expert's testimony or expertise, you will upset the Judge.

But it could get even worse. Asking the wrong question here could also elicit an answer from the medical expert that convinces the Judge to deny your claim. You will not win the case by fighting with a qualified medical expert, but you could, and likely will, both upset the Judge and say something detrimental to your claim. I will once again stress that this is why you need a representative with you at the hearing.

A medical expert may also testify in a way that is helpful to your claim. However, you have to recognize when a doctor is providing helpful testimony, and an unrepresented claimant may not. You have to know when and how to push back, and when to let it go. Since you do not have the knowledge or skill set of a qualified representative, you need to hire someone who has this knowledge, or you may make a terrible mistake. So, if you do not have a representative with you, all you can do is let the doctor and the Judge have their discussion, and wait patiently for your turn to testify. Don't worry, you're next!

In most cases, there will be no medical expert appearing at the hearing, so the claimant will be the first to testify. The Judge will begin with a handful of basic questions, such as height, weight, what type of home the claimant lives in, are there stairs, whether the claimant is working, easy stuff. Each Judge has their own way of starting the claimant's testimony, but none of this is difficult. A claimant should not overthink any of this, and certainly should not start acting. It will not help your case if, in your response to the question of whether your home has stairs, you tell the Judge "I don't understand" or "I don't remember."

Do not try to fool a Social Security Judge by telling the Judge you don't know the answer to something if you really do. What will happen is that the Judge will say you refused to cooperate. Your claim will either be dismissed or the Judge will issue an unfavorable decision citing your unwillingness to actively and honestly participate in the hearing. People do try this, and it never works. The Judge will get to your impairments and symptoms, at which point you can explain difficulty understanding, concentrating, remembering, etc., but don't play games. This is a serious proceeding, and the Judge will not tolerate any antics. Treat the Judge and the process with respect and honestly do your best.

Having said that, I want to stress that "I don't know" or "I cannot recall" may sometimes be an acceptable answer, but not always. When the Judge asks about your birthday, tell the Judge your birthday, don't say "I don't know" or "I can't remember." But if, later on, the Judge asks how many times you went to the Emergency Room in 2019, of course you can say "I cannot recall" if that is the truth. If you went several times, and the Judge knows this because it's all in your medical records, the Judge will know that is a reasonable answer. But it is not reasonable to start feigning loss of memory for your name or birthday. Yes, some people will do this, and the Judges have no patience for it. If you do that, it will be an easy denial for the Judge.

Once all of the introductory questions are out of the way, the Judge will start to ask you the questions you have been waiting over a year to answer. Some Judges prefer open-ended questions such as "Tell me why you can't work" while others will ask very specific questions about each particular impairment indicated in the medical record. Such questions might sound something like this: "So I see you had left knee surgery in 2019. Once you had fully recovered, how many hours in an eight hour workday could have you stood while working and staying on task?" Most Judges, however, will begin with broad, general questions, and then ask follow-up questions throughout the claimant's testimony.

The testimony will normally have a very conversational back-and-forth nature to it, but don't be fooled into thinking the Judge is on your side. Sometimes the Judge is truly trying to learn more about the claimant's condition and fill in gaps in the evidence, but many times the Judge has already made a decision in the case, and is simply trying to build a record of testimony to utilize in the written decision. And even if the Judge is nice, that decision might be unfavorable.

The Judge will likely be very familiar with the evidence. Even though the Judge has likely only looked through the medical records for around one hour, the Social Security Judges and Attorney Advisor decision writers are highly skilled at reviewing and interpreting medical records. This allows the Judges to use their time very efficiently, meaning they can learn a lot about a claimant by skillfully locating the most pertinent evidence in the record. Any inconsistencies are surely going to come up during the hearing, and a representative can help a claimant be prepared for those questions.

After the claimant testifies, the Judge will typically call any other witnesses at the claimant's request (family, friends, colleagues, etc.). However, to be honest, the Judges place very little value on these statements. These are merely observations and opinions, and they carry very little weight in the eyes of most Judges because they are non-medical opinions from non-medical sources. For this reason, the Judges consider these opinions less persuasive than the reports of treating doctors, objective medical studies such as x-rays and MRI reports, and testimony from reviewing medical experts.

104

17. The Vocational Expert's Testimony

The final person to provide testimony is the vocational expert. You learned about that person earlier during the introduction of all the hearing participants. Because the vocational expert's testimony is so critical to your hearing, this discussion requires its own chapter.

I have already explained that the vocational expert will be asked a series of supposedly hypothetical questions, involving physical and mental limitations of a person who does not exist. I have introduced to you the concept of hypothetical scenarios, and I have explained why the Judge asks questions to the vocational expert in this manner. By now, you know that the Judge needs to know, for each hypothetical scenario, whether the hypothetical person can do any of the claimant's past relevant work, or any other work that exists in significant numbers in the national economy.

But now I want to explain more about these hypothetical scenarios. In fact, by now you may have figured out that they are not truly *hypothetical* at all. The Judge is not making up the limitations out of thin air. The Judge has reviewed your medical records. The Judge has a good idea of your alleged impairments, and how well supported each impairment is. So, while the Judge will call these hypothetical scenarios, they are, in fact, based on the medical evidence in the record.

While the limitations do come from the claimant's medical records, technically speaking, the testimony is not about you, the claimant, but about a hypothetical person the Judge makes up. The hypothetical person appears very similar to you and has a lot of the same limitations you have, but the Judge may say that the hypothetical person can do something you don't think you can do. Or, the hypothetical person may even be more limited than you are.

We know this person is a hypothetical person because the Judge will often change the circumstances of the hypothetical scenario and ask the vocational expert to re-evaluate what work the hypothetical person can do. Sometimes the Judge will provide just one hypothetical scenario, and other times there will be several, with small changes each time. The Judge does this to assess the specific impact of each limitation on the occupations the hypothetical person could do.

Tinkering with the hypothetical scenario allows the Judge to see how the changes being made will impact the occupations the person could do. This gives the Judge a preview of what the decision *might* look like. Here is an example. Let's say the Judge finds the hypothetical person has limitations A, B, and C, and the vocational expert says that such a hypothetical person could do occupations X, Y, and Z. But then the Judge adds limitation D, and in response, the vocational expert testifies that all occupations are eliminated. This lets the Judge know that the factor which would result in a favorable decision is in fact limitation D, because someone with that limitation cannot do any occupations. This tells the Judge that to approve the claim, the RFC must include limitation D. This is one way the Judge can use the hypothetical scenarios to determine where the line is between finding the claimant disabled or not disabled.

During the vocational expert's testimony, you might hear the Judge say something like this: "For hypothetical #2, please consider all of the same limitations from hypothetical #1, but add that the claimant cannot bend or stoop at all. How does that change what occupations the hypothetical person could do?" In this case, "limitation D," the factor that would swing the outcome of the

106

decision, is not being able to bend or stoop. In theory, the Judge has not yet decided the outcome of the case, but changing the hypothetical scenario and learning from the vocational expert how that would impact the outcome tells the Judge precisely where the line is between approval and denial of benefits. The Judge is thinking, "If I find limitation D, this changes the outcome. What if I find limitation E, or F, what happens then?" The only way the Judge can know for sure is to change the hypothetical scenarios posed to the vocational expert and listen for the answer as to how the available occupations may change.

While you do not know yet what specific limitations the Judge will find in your specific RFC, most likely one of the hypothetical scenarios posed to the vocational expert will be the specific series of limitations the Judge is planning to put into the written decision. The reason is that the Judge needs to cite the vocational expert's testimony in the decision as evidence that the claimant can do past relevant work (Step 4) or that there are, or are not, a significant number of jobs in the national economy that the claimant can perform (Step 5). A fully favorable decision can actually be made without this evidence, but most Judges will gather it anyway.

But how does the vocational expert know whether a person with a given set of physical and/or mental limitations can perform a specific occupation? The answer comes from various publications issued by the United States Department of Labor. The main source the vocational expert will cite is called the Dictionary of Occupational Titles, or DOT. The DOT has not been revised in over 30 years. It still contains references to telegraph machines, fax machines, and elevator operators, and almost no references to a modern, internet-based economy. The information the vocational expert uses never changes, and the Judges and vocational experts know each other well since they work together all the time. So, when the Judge offers a *hypothetical* scenario, the vocational expert often knows which three occupations the Judge is looking for, and the Judge often knows which three occupations the vocational expert will cite.

After providing the name of the occupation, the vocational expert will cite the occupation's nine digit DOT code, will indicate the exertion level of the occupation (sedentary, light, or medium work), will indicate the Specific Vocational Preparation (SVP), and will say how many of these jobs there are in the national economy. Let's explore each of these pieces of information separately.

The nine digit DOT code is a unique identification number. Each occupation has its own unique code, which tells the Judge information about the occupation, such as what category it falls under. For example, professional athlete is under the category of entertainment. Next comes the exertion level, which as you already know defines how much sitting, standing, lifting, carrying, bending, and stooping the occupation involves. You also already know the vocational expert will testify to the specific number of jobs for the occupation that exist in the national economy. The final piece of information is the SVP. This number indicates the amount of time it takes to learn to do the job to an average performance level, a concept I introduced earlier. The SVP ranges from 1 to 9, with the higher numbers indicating more skilled jobs that take longer to learn to do.

Here is an example of what you might hear at the hearing after the Judge presents a hypothetical set of work related limitations and asks the vocational expert if there are any occupations such a hypothetical person could do. The vocational expert might say, "The hypothetical person could do work such as *cashier II*, DOT number 211.462-010, light work, SVP 2, with 1,000,000 jobs in the national economy."

This is a lot of information, presented very quickly. So, let's break it down. "Cashier II" is the title of the occupation in the DOT. This is followed by the nine digit DOT number. "Light work" is the exertional level, indicating that cashiers typically stand most of the day. There are 1,000,000 such jobs around the country. The final piece of information, "SVP 2," indicates the job is unskilled and can be learned within 30 days. Once again, I strongly recommend the presence of a qualified representative who knows how to quickly interpret vocational expert testimony, as this information will come quickly, and you need someone by your side who can decode the vocational expert's testimony, understand it right away, and be ready to ask a follow-up question.

As I mentioned earlier, at least one of the hypothetical scenarios presented by the Judge will likely be the RFC the Judge will place into the written decision. But how does the Judge come up with the RFC? It is based on the medical evidence, of course. Right? Well, there must be evidence to justify the RFC, but the truth is that most evidence can be translated into any number of different work related limitations. For example, an MRI report showing moderate degeneration in the lumbar spine can be used to justify essentially any limitation, from the ability to do medium work lifting 50 pounds, right down to having so much pain the person could not do any full time work. The same impairment can impact different people in very different ways.

In practice, what this means is that the Judge can take almost any record and find a way to either approve or deny the claim, making the decision first and working backwards to find the supporting logic and justification. If the Judge wants to find the person disabled, the Judge can say that claimant would be in so much pain that the person would not be able to complete a full time work schedule. Conversely, if the Judge wants to find the 48-year-old plumber with back pain that we met in Chapter 10 not disabled, the Judge can find that the person can do sedentary, or light, or shockingly, even medium work! The Judge can use the vocational expert's testimony to pose a series of hypothetical scenarios to find out exactly where the line is between approval and denial, and can then decide which side of that line to land on.

In fact, the Judges know the DOT occupations so well, that in most cases, they know which limitations will preclude which occupations. This means the Judges do not need to ask the vocational expert the same questions in every hearing. The requirements of the various occupations never change. So, a Judge who knows he wants to find that the claimant can go back to being a cashier (at Step 4), for example, knows he has to find that the person can stand most of the day, otherwise that job will be eliminated.

It's not just the vocational experts and the Judges who know the DOT well. The attorneys who draft the decisions also learn the physical and mental requirements of various occupations. All it takes is repetition. You tell me the age of the claimant and the RFC, and that is all the information I need to tell you whether the vocational expert will be able to cite occupations at the hearing that will have a significant number of jobs. Sometimes education and skills learned during prior work experience also play a part, but those cases are rare. For most cases, the only relevant issues are the RFC and the age of the claimant.

For a claimant under age 50, the ability to do sedentary work (even if none actually exists where you live) will generally mean the

110

person is not disabled. For a claimant under age 55, the same rule exists, but only if the person can do light work activity. Above age 55, the person would need to be able to do medium work for the case to be a slam dunk denial. As a person ages, and gets closer to retirement age, SSA rules become complex, and each person's individual circumstances need to be evaluated more closely. I will explain this more in Chapter 18.

The fact that SSA rules and the requirements for various occupations haven't changed in 30 years is the reason your Judge may only provide the vocational expert with a single hypothetical scenario. The Judge knows those limitations will be sufficient to confirm three occupations, a significant number of jobs, and a denial of benefits. The Judge does not need to inquire further once there is sufficient evidence to support the decision the Judge wants to issue. After the Judge is done asking questions, your representative can also pose hypothetical scenarios to the vocational expert, but it's the Judge who decides what limitations will go into the RFC in the decision.

So, if the Judge is set on denying the claim, there is not much your representative can do at that point in the hearing to avoid a denial. However, your representative can expand the record by obtaining additional vocational expert testimony. Perhaps that might convince the Judge to make a different decision. Otherwise, that additional evidence could be used for an appeal. I will cover appeals in Chapter 20.

If you are unrepresented, things get complicated. Many unrepresented claimants find it difficult to understand the purpose of the vocational expert at the hearing. As a result, unrepresented claimants often have tremendous difficulty when it's their turn to ask questions to the vocational expert. As was the case with the medical expert(s), if the claimant does not have a representative, once the Judge is done asking questions, the unrepresented claimant will be able to ask questions. But in order to ask effective questions, the unrepresented claimant has to understand the vocational expert's testimony, and most unrepresented claimants do not.

When an unrepresented claimant hears three occupations listed by the vocational expert, many then ask, "Are you saying I can do those jobs?" This is, of course, not what the vocational expert was saying at all. All the vocational expert does is evaluate the list of limitations set forth by the Judge, and identify whether that hypothetical person can do the claimant's past relevant work or any other work that exists in significant numbers in the national economy. However, many unrepresented claimants simply do not understand that the vocational expert is not passing judgment on them, but is instead just responding to the hypothetical scenarios posed by the Judge.

This often leads to questions that are outside the scope of the expert's testimony or expertise, which the Judge will not allow. Many cases are decided based on the what the vocational expert says. An experienced representative can help ensure that the right questions are asked, and that the vocational expert's answers are as helpful as possible for the claimant.

Alright, enough doom and gloom. Now for some good news. The Judge's familiarity with SSA rules and with the requirements of various occupations means that it is also fairly easy for Judges to approve claims. That is, when they want to! Almost any medical condition can produce pain and/or difficulty concentrating. That allows any Judge with almost any record to decide, in a fully supported manner, that the person could not sustain a traditional 40 hour per week work schedule.

112

To get to a favorable decision, the Judge could find that you have significant difficulty with any of the following: showing up for work; staying on task throughout the work shift; being able to understand, remember, and carry out simple instructions; being able to have at least minimal supervision; being able to get along (at least superficially) with other workers; being able to make simple workplace judgments; or being able to deal with basic, routine changes to the work setting. Or, the Judge could decide that you could not sit, stand, and walk for a combined total of eight hours per workday. Or perhaps the Judge might say you need to lie down periodically throughout the workday. There are so many ways to approve a case, depending on the nature of your impairments. And I have more good news! The Judge can make any of these findings without needing testimony from a vocational expert. So, if the Judge ends the hearing without the vocational expert testifying, in all likelihood you just won your case!

18. The Grid Rules – And How Judges Get Around Them

For people over 50, there are times when SSA regulations will outright declare a person to be disabled. The "grid rules" are essentially just a big chart that tells the Judge when there is discretion and when the Judge is required to find someone "disabled." These rules are complicated, and you need to have a qualified representative decipher them for you.

In order for you to understand how these rules work, there are some basic principles you need to know. The general rule is that you should be found disabled by the Judge if you cannot do your past relevant work, and either you are 50 years of age and limited to sedentary work, or you are 55 years of age and limited to sedentary or light work. If the Judge finds that you can do medium work, you're age doesn't matter. The combined number of jobs at the sedentary, light, and medium exertional levels throughout the national economy is so great that the grid rules do not direct a Judge to find a person disabled if the person can do medium work, regardless of age.

If the applicable grid rule dictates that you are disabled, the Judge must follow that rule at Step 5 of the sequential evaluation process and approve your claim. The rationale here is that as you approach retirement age, it becomes more and more difficult to transition to other jobs you have not done during the past 15 years. This is good news for claimants. But first the Judge has to eliminate all of your past relevant work at Step 4.

Here is an example of how this might work. Let's say the claimant's only past relevant work is cashier, which we know is light work because it involves a lot of standing. If the claimant is a 50-

year-old person who is limited to sedentary work, the Judge knows such a person cannot do a job involving a lot of standing. Do you see how the Judge knows the vocational expert's answer before the question is even asked? The Judge knows this work will be precluded at Step 4. Still, the Judge needs to pose that scenario so that the vocational expert can provide the expected answer, as that evidence is necessary to eliminate the past work at Step 4 and approve your claim using the grid rule at Step 5.

But there is no guarantee that you will be approved. The Judge can still deny a claim even if the claimant is in their early 60s. If SSA regulations indicate that you should be found disabled at Step 5 of the sequential evaluation process, the Judge can go back to Step 4 and rethink your past work to see if there is a job you could do despite your impairments. The Judge will need to identify what qualifies as past relevant work, and will need to ask the vocational expert whether a hypothetical person with your limitations can do that work. If the answer is yes for any past job, the Judge could deny the claim. And because that is Step 4, the Judge does not need to find that there are a significant number of jobs, just that you could perform past relevant work.

Using the prior example, for a denial of benefits, the Judge could simply change the scenario to a 50-year-old person who can do light work. Then, the vocational expert would testify that the person could do the cashier job. Since that job is past relevant work, the Judge now has the evidence necessary to deny the claim at Step 4. As you can see, the Judge is not passively listening during your hearing. The Judge is actively thinking about whether to approve or deny your claim, and what evidence is needed from the vocational expert in order to do that in the written decision. As I said, consideration of the grid rules does not start until the claimant reaches age 50, when those grid rules begin to direct the Judge to find you disabled under certain specific circumstances.

If your past relevant work is definitely outside the scope of the RFC, the Judge has one other denial tool. The Judge can use something called "transferability of skills" to deny your claim. This is a Step 5 finding that is built into the grid rules. If you have skilled past relevant work, the Judge can find that you have acquired some skills doing that work that would transfer to other work that exists in significant numbers in the national economy. Therefore, even though you cannot do your past relevant work anymore, you may have acquired some skills that could transfer to a job that is within the RFC.

In such a circumstance, the grid rules do not require that you be found disabled, even at age 50 even if you are limited to sedentary work, or at age 55 if you are limited to light work. The rules for transferable skills are incredibly complex, so if you are over the age of 50 and you have skilled past relevant work, you need a qualified representative to help you avoid being denied on this basis.

Let's return to the 48-year-old plumber from Chapter 10 one final time. At age 48, he is not disabled even if he can do only light or sedentary work. This is because, while he could not be a plumber anymore, he could do other, less physically strenuous work that exists in significant numbers in the national economy. Again, this does *not* mean that he will ever be able to find such work or be successful at such work. This is a theoretical conclusion that he *could* do work that exists in significant numbers throughout the United States, and that's all the Judge needs to find in order to deny this disability claim.

But now let's say the plumber is 58 instead of 48. The only job this person did in the past 15 years is plumber, which is medium

116

work. If the plumber's back disorder limits him to sedentary or light work, the applicable grid rule directs the Judge to find the plumber disabled. The only difference between now and earlier in the book is the claimant's age. As he got older, he had a better chance of being found disabled. As a 48-year-old, the claimant had little chance of approval, but 10 years later, at age 58, he is approved. Age is therefore the key difference between a successful and unsuccessful claim in this example. This is the purpose of the grid rules, to require that Judges find older claimants disabled because those claimants would have the most difficulty transitioning to other work in the national economy.

But let's say the Judge wants to deny this claim for some reason, even for a 58-year-old former plumber. Perhaps he thinks the plumber is lying about something, or he sees in the record that the plumber likes to engage in a strenuous activity. Perhaps the record reflects that one time the claimant went ice skating, or that he sometimes likes to do a little gardening. An activity mentioned once in the record does not show that a claimant can do a strenuous job for 40 hours per week on an ongoing basis. However, if the Judge *really* wants to find the person not disabled, the Judge can cling to something like this and run with it. Judges do this all the time.

Often a Judge will cling to a random comment and cite it numerous times throughout the decision. "Well, he can do gardening, which involves bending, so clearly he can do medium work activity." I wrote over 1,800 decisions during more than seven years as an Attorney Advisor decision writer, and I did this more times than I care to remember. This was part of the job. Do you remember what my former supervisor told me about the Judges? "You write what they want, not what you want." And sometimes, what they wanted was a decision that points to something the claimant did one time and uses that as justification for something completely different. Doing gardening one time does not mean a person can work as a plumber!

Many times, such a comment would be found in a single medical record, where the person ended up needing to seek treatment for pain due to having engaged in the activity! For example, I would see an Emergency Room record explaining that the person tried to do something active, like gardening, one time. This activity was mentioned in that record because the person sustained a back injury *while* gardening and needed emergency treatment. Rather than point out that such an activity caused pain, which shows the claimant could not do that activity on an ongoing basis, I would be told by the Judge to cite that single mention of gardening (in a 1,000 page medical record) as proof that the claimant is clearly exaggerating symptoms. It makes no sense, yet it happens all the time. This is how Judges take records that heavily favor the claimant and create unfavorable decisions. They ignore the truth in favor of an alternate narrative that suits their desire to deny the claim.

Let's go back to our now 58-year-old plumber. Let's assume the claimant is limited to light work due to a limited ability to bend. Since the claimant's past work as a plumber is considered medium work, at Step 5 of the sequential evaluation process, the grid rules would direct a finding that the claimant is disabled. But let's assume, for whatever reason, the Judge really wants to deny this claim. Since the Judge cannot do so at Step 5, he will simply return to Step 4 and more closely re-examine the claimant's past relevant work. If the Judge finds a job the claimant has done in the past that fits all the elements of past relevant work (done at SGA, within the past 15 years, SVP is satisfied), the Judge will simply change the RFC to make sure the limitations in the decision match the requirements of

118

the claimant's past job. That way, once the vocational expert confirms the past job is possible with that hypothetical set of limitations, the Judge can deny the claim at Step 4. It's starting with the end in mind, and working your way back to find justification for the conclusion you want. Judges do this often.

We know the plumber job is eliminated because it is medium work, requiring a lot of bending. But perhaps the plumber worked as a cashier for six weeks during one holiday season to make some extra money to buy gifts. Or maybe during an economic downturn several years ago, business was slow, so the plumber took a job for a couple months as a cashier in a hardware store. This is fairly common. Seldom does a person have only one job during the past 15 years. These other jobs are light work, so the Judge can find the person can do light work and that would be sufficient for a denial at Step 4. If, on the other hand, the only past job done within the past 15 years is the plumber job, and the Judge wants to deny the claim, the Judge would need to find that the person can do medium work. Or, the Judge could decide to just approve the claim and move on, which does sometimes happen.

But if, during the past 15 years, you worked a job that did not involve a substantial amount of lifting, carrying, or bending, the Judge may very well find that you can do such light work, and deny your claim, even if you are in your early 60s. You may have done the work for just a short period 14 years ago, and yet this can cause your claim to be denied. This decision is not realistic because you won't be going back to that job. If you could do that, you would have already. But SSA regulations are not trying to help you find a new career. They are simply asking whether, *in theory*, there is an occupation that you could perform. The Social Security Disability regulations do not care about reality, just what you theoretically could do assuming the Judge's RFC is completely accurate. It likely isn't, you likely can't do that job, and it may not even exist where you live.

I know that, but the regulations don't care. A Judge who wants to deny your claim will find a reason to do so. You can appeal the RFC finding, saying it is not supported by the evidence. And you can appeal a Step 4 denial based on a job you did 16 years ago because that is an objective error of law. But you cannot appeal a finding that says you can go back to a job that you did 14 years ago simply because you don't like that finding. That is exactly how the law defines Step 4. It is a legitimate way to deny a claim, and it is mostly used when the claimant is over age 50 if the person would otherwise be found disabled at Step 5. The law puts Step 4 there for a reason. I am sorry, this is just how the law is written.

So, for the plumber, if there is other past work, like cashier, the Judge can issue a decision finding the person can do light work, and deny the claim. If there is no past work other than plumber, the Judge can use the single comment about gardening to say the person can do medium work, and can either continue being a plumber, or can do other medium work that exists in significant numbers in the national economy. Even if that is not true, many Judges will do it anyway. There is no one to tell them no. They are independent, they do what they want. And the best part for them is that someone else has to write the decision and formulate all of the logic to prop up their irrational, illogical, and unsupported findings.

But how can a person possibly be found capable of medium work, which involves a lot of bending, if the person has a severe back impairment? The answer is of the "because I said so" variety. All the Judge has to do is declare that the plumber's back impairment leaves that person able to do medium work, and voila,

120

the vocational expert will testify that a similar hypothetical person can perform the requirements of the claimant's past work as a plumber, which of course the Judge knows will be the evidence needed to issue an unfavorable decision.

As I have said throughout this book, many Judges begin by knowing what needs to be true in order to deny a claim. The Judge then looks for that evidence. If it is not found anywhere in the record, the Judge can call a medical expert to testify at the hearing, can creatively interpret the medical records, or can make supported inferences. The Judge can also obtain vocational evidence to support a denial. The Judge could present a hypothetical scenario to the vocational expert knowing it will match past relevant work or other work that exists in significant numbers in the national economy. That evidence can then be used to deny the claim.

Absent new evidence from a medical expert, the evidence did not change, the law did not change, and the claimant's medical condition did not change. The only change here occurred in the Judge's brain. The Judge decided to take that record and make it a denial, and then went ahead and did it. Do you remember when I said that the five steps of the sequential evaluation process are followed in order? Well, that is how we are told the process is supposed to work. But, as you now see, in reality, the Judge gets to mentally skip ahead and decide the outcome of the case, then move back and do the steps in order but with a very specific conclusion in mind.

Regardless of whether the plumber is 48 or 58, the Judge can use the same evidence to decide the case either way. While the steps are supposed to be followed in order, in practical terms, most cases are decided by how the Judge feels and by what the Judge wants. The five-step rationale is then not for the purpose of reaching the conclusion, but for the purpose of justifying the conclusion that has already been reached.

19. After the Hearing

After the hearing, the Judge will, at some point during the following several weeks, prepare instructions for the decision to be drafted. Some Judges do this right after the hearing, and some even during the hearing! But most wait until after the hearing, possibly the same day, possibly later that week. They may also need to wait for additional evidence to come in after the hearing. This is particularly true if the claimant or the representative indicated an expectation of new evidence possibly arriving at some point after the hearing. Perhaps there was some difficulty getting medical records, or maybe the claimant had a recent procedure done.

Once the record is complete, the Judge will use SSA shorthand to create internal decision drafting instructions. The Judge will then use the SSA case management system to indicate that the case is ready to be assigned to an Attorney Advisor decision writer so the decision can be drafted. Sometimes the case will then sit for days or weeks, depending on how backed-up the office is. The case may also be transferred to an SSA decision writing unit somewhere else in the country, meaning the Judge has no idea who will actually be drafting their decision.

Once the case is finally ready for drafting, a manager will assign the case to an Attorney Advisor decision writer, who will review the medical record, the hearing recording, and the Judge's shorthand instructions. The instructions tell the Attorney Advisor decision writer whether the decision is to be fully favorable, unfavorable, or only partially favorable to the claimant. If partially favorable, the instructions will indicate whether the decision is a *later onset* decision or a *closed period* decision, as discussed in Chapter 5. The instructions will also indicate what step of the sequential evaluation process the decision should end at, how medical and other opinion evidence should be evaluated, and whether drug or alcohol use will impact the decision (which I will discuss in Chapter 26). The instructions can run several pages, but an efficient Judge can do it in one page, using one sentence or less for each piece of information.

SSA shorthand truly is its own language, and employees need to be trained in how to encode and decipher messages. An RFC in the decision instructions that the Judge sends to the Attorney Advisor decision writer might look something like this: "UF/5. Light, s/w 4, sit 4, freq RS, occ LRS, SRRT, simple WPC, occ CW con." If you are confused, I don't blame you. But let's go item by item and I will explain to you what the Judge is telling the Attorney Advisor decision writer to do.

The Judge begins by indicating the decision will be unfavorable and will be decided at Step 5. The Judge wants the decision to reflect that the claimant can do light work, which is defined in the regulations as the ability to lift 20 pounds frequently (up to two thirds of a workday) and 10 pounds occasionally (up to one third of a workday). The claimant can stand and/or walk not six hours per workday, as the regulations define light work, but in this specific case only four hours, while sitting the other four hours of a standard eight hour workday. The claimant can frequently climb ramps and stairs, but can only occasionally climb ladders, ropes, and scaffolds. The claimant can engage in simple, routine, repetitive tasks, with simple workplace changes, but can only have occasional contact with co-workers. Do you see how efficient the shorthand can be? Judges and Attorney Advisor decision writers are all trained on these terms so they can understand each other. This is how a complex decision with a lengthy medical record can be boiled down to a single page of instructions.

When I was an Attorney Advisor decision writer, I could review decision instructions and know within 20 seconds what the decision was going to be, what medical opinions would be in the evidence, what the Judge thinks of that evidence, and why the decision is going to be laid out in a particular way. This does not mean that the instructions are perfect, far from it. Judges move quickly, spending only about an hour on each medical record, and some records have thousands of pages of medical evidence to review. So, part of the Attorney Advisor decision writer's job is locating any evidence that may have been missed, particularly if there is a medical opinion that the Judge did not discuss and evaluate in the decision instructions.

This is especially important if the located evidence contradicts something that is supposed to be in the decision, or if the new evidence might possibly change the outcome of the decision. In such a circumstance, the Attorney Advisor decision writer will need to bring this newly identified evidence to the Judge. Some Judges want to also have a recommendation presented to them, while others make it very clear over time that the opinion of the Attorney Advisor decision writer is not valued. This is unfortunate since the job title is Attorney *Advisor,* meaning it is literally in the job title and job description to advise the Judges. However, some Judges just do not want to hear anyone else's opinion. "Don't question my decision, just write it."

For the Judges who do want input from the Attorney Advisor decision writer, the attorney will analyze the new evidence, usually in an e-mail, and will give the Judge time to review their notes, their instructions, the evidence, and the attorney's recommendation for how to handle the evidence. The Judge will then send back an amended instruction regarding what to do with the newly identified evidence.

The Attorney Advisor decision writer can approach management if they feel the Judge is not acting fairly or rationally, but management will always side with the Judge. I was once given instructions that directly defied the evidence, SSA regulations, and basic logic. When I brought this to a manager, I was told "If you feel you cannot draft this decision, we will find someone else who can." What I learned was, in the end, the Judge gets the last word. For the Attorney Advisor decision writer, it's best to do what the Judge says, as best you can, using all of your knowledge, skill, and artistic ability, and then move on to the next case.

Once the decision draft is complete, the Attorney Advisor decision writer sends the decision draft to the Judge to review and edit. As I indicated in Chapter 14, the Judge can return the case to management to have it sent back to the Attorney Advisor decision writer if the Judge feels the instructions were not fully or properly followed. Sadly, many of the slowest Judges will use this tactic just to clear cases out of their queue so they are not blamed for these languishing cases. These Judges, who simply cannot handle the size of the workload or the speed of the job, would send cases back to management, indicating their instructions were not followed. But it is often their own inability to do the job that should be re-examined, not the decision draft.

Bad instructions, poor analysis, missed evidence, sending cases back to the attorneys, and passing blame onto everyone else, these are the hallmarks of the worst Judges. All the Attorney Advisors can do is take the stale, rotten ingredients they are given

126

and try to make the best, most appetizing decision possible. It isn't easy!

Luckily, many of these Judges do not last long. While these tactics can get a Judge through weeks, or possibly even months, the job requirements do eventually catch up with them, and they end up changing their ways. They start moving faster, being more efficient, and respecting their attorney colleagues, or they are simply pushed out. Not literally, but after enough emails telling you that you are too slow, that you need additional training, that your telework is being suspended, that you are not meeting your assigned goal, etc., eventually it just wears these Judges down and they decide they cannot deal with it anymore. When they do eventually leave, it comes as a huge relief to the Attorney Advisors.

Back to our case timeline. The Judge has written instructions, and the attorney has drafted the decision. The Judge has reviewed and edited the decision, and has finalized it with an electronic signature. Management then closes the case in the electronic case management system. Finally, a paper copy of the decision is mailed to the claimant and the representative. The hearing level is now complete.

20. The Appeals Process

If the decision is fully favorable, the claimant will be happy. The claimant will be getting all the benefits to which the claimant is entitled. However, even after a fully favorable decision, the claimant will need to wait 60 days before benefits can start. This is also when the claimant's representative will be paid. The claimant may also get a lump sum amount of past due benefits for the time when the claimant was disabled but was not receiving benefits because the case was in process. The representative's fee comes out of these past due benefits only, and remember it is capped at 25% or $6,000 (increasing to $7,200 in November 2022), whichever is smaller.

Alright, now for the unpleasant part. What happens when the decision is not fully favorable to the claimant? If the decision is unfavorable, moving forward is easy: you appeal. Even if you think you have no grounds to appeal, you and your representative find the one or two best arguments and you assert them as best you can. The Judges and Attorney Advisor decision writers move very quickly, and as hard as they try, there are always gaps in the work. Medical opinions are not analyzed as thoroughly as they could be, the claimant's allegations may be misconstrued, or perhaps the Judge completely missed an opinion, or an imaging study, or a blood test.

Something, anything, can work for an appeal. You have nothing to lose. You might as well try and see if maybe you can get something to stick. If you have a qualified representative, that person will usually handle the appeal to the Appeals Council. The representative can submit a list of specific errors for the Appeals Council to consider (called contentions), but the attorneys who review the decision at the Appeals Council will also review the decision and the evidence even without contentions, and often they find errors that you and your representative did not even know about.

Clearly, no one wants to receive an unfavorable decision. Almost all representatives will appeal those, because doing so requires nothing more than a one page form saying the claimant disagrees with the decision. Some representatives will also submit contentions. It's a good idea to ask the representative, before signing a fee agreement with them, how they will handle an appeal in case it comes to that. This is something you will want to know ahead of time.

Even though you hope for a favorable decision the first time around, you want to be prepared for an unfavorable decision, so if that should occur, you and the representative are on the same page with the appeal strategy. You want to know whether the representative will file only the one page form and move on to the next case, assuming your case is a loser and that it isn't worth the additional time or effort. But you also want to know if the representative believes in your case enough to spend additional time on an appeal by writing a list of contentions for the Appeals Council to review and consider.

There is a lot to think about when deciding whether or not to appeal. The claimant and representative need to carefully review the decision and weigh their options. But, the final call lies with the claimant. As I said earlier, it is the claimant's case, and the claimant decides whether to appeal. The representative can provide advice and counsel, and of course will submit the written appeal with contentions to the Appeals Council. But the claimant makes the decision to appeal.

While such a decision is easy if your claim was denied, things get more complicated if the ALJ's decision was partially favorable. Any decision that grants the claimant benefits, but fewer benefits than the claimant was seeking, is partially favorable. In such a circumstance, the claimant has a decision to make. I discussed this in Chapter 5 when explaining how the representative gets paid.

Before making any decisions, the claimant and the representative need to review the Judge's decision to determine if it is a later onset decision or a closed period decision. The decision may also be labeled "partially favorable" if it is unfavorable for Title 2, but favorable for Title 16, because the claimant was found disabled, but only after the DLI.

The claimant and the representative need to review the decision to determine why it is partially favorable, and how far below the requested level of benefit the claimant was awarded. If the decision is a later onset decision, finding the claimant disabled on October 1st when the claimant alleged that disability began on September 1st of the same year, that one month of lost benefits is probably not worth appealing.

On the other hand, three circumstances make an appeal more likely and worthwhile. First, for a later onset decision, if the EOD is a long period of time after the AOD, there would be a large unfavorable portion of the decision. Second, for a closed period decision, if benefits are cut off many years prior to the claimant reaching retirement age, this would also mean a lot of lost benefits for the claimant. Third, if the claimant is found disabled, but after the DLI, this precludes SSDI benefits entirely. In all of these circumstances, there is a lot of money at stake!

Let's review this last situation in more detail, because this is perhaps the best reason to appeal. Normally, when a partially favorable decision is appealed, the claimant needs to appeal the *entire* decision. While the representative can write appeal contentions citing error only in the portion of the decision that is unfavorable to the claimant, the entire decision will still be reviewed. It is possible that the appellate reviewer *could* then find error with the favorable portion of the decision, so there is a substantial risk to pursuing such an appeal.

However, there is less risk when the decision is labeled "partially favorable" specifically because the claimant is found disabled, but after the DLI. This decision is not actually partially favorable. Instead, it is actually two separate decisions: an unfavorable Title 2 decision and a favorable Title 16 decision. This situation can only occur if the DLI is in the past, since the Judge found that the claimant's disability began *after* the DLI. The one positive part about such a decision is that because these are two distinct decisions, the claimant can appeal the Title 2 unfavorable decision without putting the Title 16 favorable decision in jeopardy. The claimant can do this by indicating this is an appeal of *only* the Title 2 decision.

Here is an example of this situation. The claimant files a claim for both SSDI and SSI benefits. The claimant's DLI was June 30, 2019. The claimant alleges that disability began on May 1, 2019, before the DLI. Note the DLI is in the past. Because the claimant is saying disability began prior to the DLI, the claimant would be eligible for SSDI benefits as well as SSI benefits. The Judge will hold a hearing and review the medical record, using the same evidence to assess both claims. After the hearing, the Judge finds the claimant disabled, but not until August 1, 2019. The Judge labels the decision "partially favorable" because the claimant is not getting all benefits which the claimant is asking for. At the bottom of the decision, just above the Judge's signature, it says the claimant was not disabled prior to the DLI, June 30, 2019, so SSDI benefits are denied, while SSI benefits are approved starting August 1, 2019.

Even though the claimant was found disabled just three months after the AOD, finding that the claimant became disabled *after* the DLI prevents the claimant from receiving any SSDI benefits. But the claimant has been approved for SSI benefits, and can therefore receive *something* while appealing the SSDI unfavorable decision. Even better, the claimant can appeal the SSDI unfavorable decision without the risk of losing the SSI benefits, because the SSI decision is not being appealed.

The Appeals Council also randomly selects favorable decisions to review for quality control. Therefore, any favorable decision, fully favorable or partially favorable, can also be automatically called for an appeal *to* the Appeals Council *by* the Appeals Council on its "own motion." If your decision is selected, the entire decision is being reviewed whether you like it or not. At the Appeals Council, staff will quietly review the evidence, and if they decide the favorable decision should be left alone and the claimant paid benefits, the ALJ's decision is then "effectuated," which means to be paid by a Social Security payment center. This review happens within the first 60 days following the date of the decision. The Appeals Council staff do this review behind the scenes, and you never know whether it happened. After 60 days, you start to receive your benefits. This is the reason you need to wait 60 days, even if the decision is favorable, before benefits can start.

If, however, the Appeals Council wants to step in and either change the decision or send it back to the ALJ for a new decision, they will send you a polite letter explaining why. Your representative will also receive a copy of this letter, and you or your representative will have 30 days to respond before the Appeals

Council acts. In practical terms though, unless you submit new evidence to correct the problem, whatever the Appeals Council suggests is what they will do. The good news is that sometimes they will actually change the decision to be *more* favorable! When that happens, they usually do not let you know in advance, they just send you the new decision letting you know you are entitled to more benefits than you previously thought. Yay!

Now let's discuss who actually works at the Appeals Council, which is located near Washington, D.C. In an Appeals Council office, there are case technicians, attorneys, managers, and Judges. All of these staff members do basically the same thing as their hearing office counterparts, but some have different titles. Group Supervisors are called Branch Chiefs at the Appeals Council, and the Hearing Office Director is called the Division Director at the Appeals Council. At the Appeals Council, however, the managers get paid more, which is interesting, since it's basically the same job.

The case technicians, attorneys, and Judges all get paid basically the same as their hearing office counterparts. At the Appeals Council, the Judges are called Administrative Appeals Judges (AAJs). However, they are not the only *adjudicators*. There is a role at the Appeals Council that does not exist at the hearing level: Appeals Officer. The Appeals Officer is a quasi-Judge. Appeals Officers are allowed to decide cases at the Appeals Council, but only in a very limited way.

Do you remember when I explained in Chapter 13 that the Appeals Council is not required by law to even exist? This means they can choose to exercise jurisdiction over a case that is appealed, or they can decline to do so and just leave it alone. If the Appeals Council wishes to accept jurisdiction, and either make a decision in the case or send it back to the ALJ for a new decision, then two

AAJs will get involved. They will review the ALJ decision and the medical record, and they will decide what to do. If, however, after reviewing the appeal, the Appeals Council wants to just leave the ALJ's decision alone, then one Appeals Officer *or* one AAJ will sign a document telling the claimant that the Appeals Council has chosen not to intervene. The Appeals Officer can only get involved in the case if the Appeals Council is going to decline jurisdiction.

The actual wording of the notice sent to the claimant is this: "We have denied your request for review." When I first heard this statement, I thought it was wildly unfair to *not even review* the case being appealed. That seems like a blatant denial of a person's due process rights! I am pretty sure most claimants probably think the same thing when they first read those words. But as I soon learned, despite the literal meaning of the words, this phrase does not actually mean that the case wasn't looked at. You can rest assured it was reviewed, despite the poor terminology.

The attorneys at the Appeals Council are called Attorney Analysts because they do not *write* decisions. Instead, they review appeals and then write an *analysis* of the case. The analysis will include any major errors in the decision, a summary of the medical evidence, and a recommendation to leave the ALJ's decision alone or to change it. The Attorney Analyst is looking to see whether there are any errors of law that would change the outcome of the decision, and is also looking to see whether the decision is supported by substantial evidence (remember, this just means there is more than a mere scintilla of evidence to support the decision).

The attorney is *not* looking for perfection. No decision is perfect, and you now know why. With the speed that cases move through the hearing level, the Attorney Advisor decision writers cannot possibly ever achieve perfection. The Attorney Analysts are merely checking to make sure there is *enough* evidence to support the Judge's decision, and that there are no *significant* errors of law. A significant error of law is an error that would change the decision from favorable to unfavorable, or vice versa. But if the decision is unfavorable, and would stay unfavorable, the error of law is not considered to be *significant* by the Appeals Council.

Consider the following unfavorable decision at Step 5. The claimant is 49 years of age and the ALJ finds that she can do sedentary work. The decision cites three sedentary occupations that exist in significant numbers in the national economy, as noted by the vocational expert during his testimony. The claimant appeals the unfavorable decision, arguing that the Judge got her birthday wrong, and she is actually 50 years of age, not 49. Because the claimant was under age 50, the Judge did not need to focus on the claimant's past relevant work. As a result, the ALJ essentially skipped that step, and simply issued a Step 5 unfavorable decision.

However, let's presume that the ALJ did get the claimant's birthday wrong (this sometimes happens). If this 50-year-old claimant has no past relevant work, or past relevant work that is not within the sedentary RFC (perhaps it's light work), the grid rules would direct a finding that the claimant is disabled at Step 5. Since the ALJ missed this, the Appeals Council would determine this to be a *significant* error of law.

Why? In this case, with the correct birthday and age, we see that the outcome of the case completely changes, it should actually be favorable. In that case, the Appeals Council needs to intervene, accept jurisdiction of the case, and could issue its own favorable decision, approving the claim for benefits. Or, it could send the case back to the ALJ for a new hearing and a new decision, telling the

ALJ to re-consider Step 4 of the sequential evaluation process, this time for a 50-year-old claimant.

But now let's change the scenario and say the claimant has sedentary past relevant work. Perhaps the ALJ did not care because at age 49 there was no reason to do a thorough Step 4 analysis when the ALJ knew that a denial would be easier to craft at Step 5. In that situation, the ALJ got lucky. The ALJ got the claimant's birthday wrong, so this was an error. However, the claimant did have sedentary past relevant work that could be done by a person with a sedentary RFC. This means the ALJ *could have* denied the claim at Step 4. Because a corrected decision would remain unfavorable (albeit at a different step in the sequential evaluation process), the Appeals Council won't step in and take action. The error is not *significant* because it does not change the overall outcome of the case. If the end result would remain the same, the Appeals Council does not find there to be a reason to intervene and to accept jurisdiction of the case. In that circumstance, the hearing level decision signed by the ALJ will become the final decision of the Commissioner of Social Security.

If the Attorney Analyst thinks the Appeals Council should accept jurisdiction of the case, it is transferred to an AAJ for review. Many of these Judges are former Appeals Officers or Attorney Analysts who are hired directly by SSA. They are paid on the same scale as the ALJs, and the hiring process is similar to the new, streamlined hiring process for ALJs. Most AAJs are already working at the Appeals Council at the time they are hired to be AAJs, resulting in a more collegial atmosphere.

The Judges are more understanding of the pressures of the Attorney Analyst role because many of them have served in that role. Also, at the Appeals Council, the Attorney Analyst reviews the case first, before the Appeals Officer or Judge, and then drafts a case analysis and a recommended outcome. This makes reviewing the case easier for the Appeals Officers and AAJs. It ensures that fewer pieces of evidence are missed or misconstrued. This is a far more positive and efficient system than the "Write what I tell you" approach at the hearing level. The result is happier workers, better decisions, and more fair outcomes.

But there is a problem with the way the Appeals Council handles cases. If the Appeals Council is going to remand the case (meaning it will go back to the hearing level for a new hearing with an ALJ and a new decision), or if the Appeals Council is going to issue a corrected decision (meaning the Appeals Council corrects some error by issuing its own decision rather than sending it back to the hearing level), you will see two AAJ signatures at the end of the document. If your case was taken up by the Appeals Council on its "own motion" and you are receiving a letter telling you why that happened, you will also see two AAJ signatures. You would then logically think that two AAJs in black robes thoroughly reviewed your case, deliberated for some time while rubbing their chins and gazing thoughtfully upward, and then arrived at a well-reasoned conclusion. You'd be wrong. While two AAJs do electronically sign the document, the amount of time that each person spends on the case varies greatly.

Here is how it actually works. If jurisdiction is being accepted by the Appeals Council, the first thing that happens is the Attorney Analyst drafts a document, which is called an "action document" because it describes the action that is about to occur. This will be one of three things. First, it could be a letter explaining the basis for jurisdiction that will be mailed to the claimant and the representative. Second, it could be a remand order sending the case back to the hearing level ALJ. Or third, it could be a new decision that will be issued by the Appeals Council.

The case analysis and the action document will then be sent to the AAJs to review. Internally, the Judges refer to themselves as the "A" Judge (the top signature) and the "B" Judge (the bottom signature). Each Judge has both "A" cases and "B" cases, but they do not spend equal amounts of time on those cases. The Judges tend to spend most of their time reviewing their "A" cases, because for those cases, that Judge is the person responsible for getting the action document ready for signature and mailing to the claimant and representative. The Judge's "B" queue is filled with cases where someone else is the "A" Judge, meaning those documents are already drafted and edited, and require only a rubber stamp approval from the "B" Judge.

For the "A" cases, the Judges tend to spend a substantial amount of time on the case, so they tend to know the evidence and legal issues in those cases well. That is not so for the "B" cases. The "B" Judge typically does not spend nearly enough time on the case to understand the legal issues, the nuances of the evidence, or why the decision is what it is. In fact, the "B" Judge may not look at the evidence at all, instead trusting that the "A" Judge made sure everything was correct.

Here is an example of how this might work. First, Attorney Analyst Alice recommends that the case of a claimant named *Calloway* be sent back to the hearing level ALJ for a new hearing and a new decision. This is called a remand, so Attorney Analyst Alice also drafts a remand order (this is the action document) which explains to the claimant, the representative, and the ALJ why the case is being sent back to the hearing level. Attorney Analyst Alice then sends the case, along with the remand order draft, to the "A"

138

Judge. Let's say we have two Judges, Judge Adams ("A") and Judge Brown ("B"). While Judge Adams is reviewing and editing the *Calloway* remand order, Judge Brown is also working on a different case where she is the "A" Judge. Both Judges are working on their own "A" case.

Once Judge Adams is done editing the draft remand order created by Attorney Analyst Alice, he moves the case to Judge Brown's "B" queue of cases. He then walks over to Judge Brown's office door, knocks twice, pokes his head in, and says "*Calloway* is ready for you." Judge Brown then pauses what she is doing, enters the *Calloway* case in the electronic case management system, and opens the draft remand order on her computer. Judge Brown makes sure the document is a remand order, makes sure it is for claimant *Calloway*, checks to see that the document is in English and that there are at least some complete sentences, and then signs the draft as the "B" Judge. I am sure some Judges take their "B" responsibilities very seriously. Sometimes the "B" Judge will even disagree with the "A" Judge and they will need to bring in a third Judge (you guessed it, the "C" Judge) to be the tie-breaker vote. But in most cases, the "B" Judge will electronically sign the document and have it out the door within just a few minutes.

When I was an Attorney Analyst at the Appeals Council, I once saw a case that I had reviewed sit with a "B" Judge for several weeks. Upon reminding the Judge that the case existed, I saw the case get signed by the "B" Judge in less than five minutes. So, we went from the Judge not even realizing this case was there to the remand order being signed in around 300 seconds. It is obvious that in such a circumstance, the "B" Judge was basically just relying on my writing and on the editing of the "A" Judge. He clearly did not spend enough time on the case to understand the evidence or to provide actual assent to the final outcome.

I am sure that all AAJs would tell you that they always spend *enough* time reviewing all of their "B" cases for accuracy. But there were times when I would approach a "B" Judge to discuss a case literally the same day the Judge signed the order, and the Judge would have absolutely no idea what I was talking about. The Judge would remember nothing about the case, and I mean nothing, not even the claimant's name! I would ask the Judge's opinion on the medical impairments, the RFC, the error in the decision, etc., and the Judge would not remember having ever reviewed that case. In those circumstances, I think the Judges feel embarrassed at being called out like that, which of course was never my intent. I am explaining all of this so you can better understand why those two Judge signatures are often a bit of a sham.

From the Appeals Council, there is only one place a case can go within SSA: back to the ALJ. Unless the case is remanded to the hearing level for a new hearing and a new ALJ decision, the Appeals Council will be your final stop within SSA. Most likely, you will receive a letter denying your Appeals Council request for review. That letter will also tell you that the ALJ's decision is the final decision of the Commissioner of Social Security. This is by far the most common scenario, with over 80% of appeals ending this way. Most of the remaining 20% are remands back to the ALJ. Rarely, the Appeals Council will issue its own decision. When that does happen, the Appeals Council's decision then becomes the final decision of the Commissioner of Social Security.

Once you receive a final decision from the Commissioner of Social Security, whether it be the ALJ's decision or an Appeals Council decision, you have three options. You can always just accept the decision and be done. If you received an unfavorable decision, this can be difficult because it means you are giving up completely on trying to claim disability benefits to which you feel you are entitled. If you do not like this option, and you want to continue to pursue benefits, you have two other options.

The next option is letting that decision go and starting over, from scratch, with a new application. There may be a risk here, though. There are certain states where having a prior unfavorable decision will hurt. Until the Supreme Court steps in and either gets rid of this rule or applies it nationwide, for now there are only certain parts of the country where this rule applies. The rule works like this: The RFC (remember, this means the *most* you can do despite your impairments) from an unfavorable decision is presumed to remain in place unless you show evidence to overcome that presumption. In other words, you have to provide really good evidence showing why that RFC was wrong. The less time between the prior unfavorable decision and the AOD of your new claim, the more evidence you need to overcome the presumption of continuing non-disability.

Here are two examples to illustrate this rule. Let's say a decision is dated March 3rd, and you then file a new claim for benefits saying you became disabled the next day, March 4th. You would need to show something *very* convincing to the new Judge for that Judge to believe that anything had changed in that one day. It is possible though. For example, let's say the day after you received the old decision, you were in a car accident. That would be pretty good evidence of a change in circumstances! That is good evidence to overcome the presumption of continuing non-disability because you would be able to show the new Judge *why* things changed since the prior decision was issued, and why you are now disabled. When you are trying to show that one day you were not disabled and literally the next day you were, you need something sudden and specific like this. Otherwise, you will not be able to overcome the presumption of continuing non-disability in such a short period.

On the other hand, if you allege you became disabled five years later, well, that is a significant amount of time, and a lot of things could have happened. In addition to normal aging, there would be over 1,800 days during which so many different things could have happened in your life to change your circumstances. This is such a long period of time that the facts from the prior decision would not apply anymore. In other words, the presumption of continuing non-disability becomes less strong over time as life events and age take a toll on mind and body. The new Judge would likely be willing to review all of the evidence during that intervening five year period and say the prior decision is too old to maintain a presumption of continuing non-disability. The new decision will then be based on evidence since the prior decision.

The purpose of this rule is to have Judges only look at a period of time once. In addition to the period before the old decision, the new Judge is allowed to presume that anything after that decision, but close in time to it, similarly does not need to be looked at again unless there is a very good reason to do so. There is a presumption that after you are found not disabled, this continues to be the case, at least for a while until you have sufficient evidence to have a new Judge make a new and fresh decision.

For efficiency of the system, it's a good rule, but it does mean that people who feel they received an unfair unfavorable decision experience a double whammy. They are not only precluded from benefits for the period *prior to* the old decision, but also for the period in the days, weeks, and even months *after* that decision, at least until they can build a sufficient medical record to support a new application for benefits.

Because of this rule, many people instead choose a third option: Fight the original unfavorable decision by taking the case to Federal Court. For this option, you would need to sue the Commissioner of Social Security in United States District Court. That's right, you would literally *make a federal case out of it!* The case has to go to Federal Court because you would be suing a federal agency. But rest assured, the whole thing is not nearly as scary as it sounds. I know someone who went through this process. She had an attorney file the case for her, help her avoid paying any fees, and the attorney did all of this without even charging for the services.

If you have a representative, your fee agreement applies to the hearing level, and possibly to the Appeals Council level. However, the fee agreement does not cover the representative's services if you end up going to Federal Court. Some Social Security Disability attorneys will not take cases to Federal Court, but they can usually refer you to someone who will. Once you find an attorney who handles Federal Court cases, you should ask how they will be paid. The great news is that the answer will likely be "by the government."

There is a law called the Equal Access to Justice Act (EAJA), which allows representatives to represent you and have the government pay them to do so. The whole point of this law is to allow for equal access to Federal Court for people with minimal financial resources. This is a fantastic law for Social Security Disability claimants, but it's an additional step in the process, and many representatives do not want to deal with the formalities of Federal Court. But for those who do, they know how this procedure works, so they can file your case and the government will pay their fee. This means there is no cost to you to access the Federal Court that *your* tax dollars pay for.

But still, "How will you get paid?" is always a good question to ask any professional before hiring their services. Even if your representative's office says they can handle your Federal Court appeal, the person who does so may be different from the person you were working with at the time of your ALJ hearing. Some offices will have one person who handles ALJ hearings and Appeals Council appeals, but someone different who handles the Federal Court cases.

For continuity of representation, it can be a good idea to hire a firm such as this, because they know you and will want to fight for you so they can get both the EAJA fee and the 25% hearing level fee. Using the same firm is also more efficient because they know your case well and they can provide you with an immediate evaluation of your options, versus having to read the hearing transcript and start from scratch. But if they instead refer you to someone else who handles Federal Court appeals, that's still okay. The fees are totally separate. That other attorney (it would need to be an attorney to file a lawsuit in Federal Court) can handle the Federal Court appeal and earn the EAJA fee, and then if your case is sent back to Social Security for a new hearing, your former representative can take over once again in pursuit of their 25% fee.

When you sue the Commissioner of Social Security, it sounds scary, but thousands of people do it each year all around the country. It's a fairly simple procedure, but it won't be anything like what you see on TV or in a movie. First, you really do need to have an attorney for this process because Federal Court is a stringent, formal place with very specific rules. Federal Judges have little tolerance for something being late or formatted incorrectly. Your

144

case might be heard by a United States District Judge appointed by the President, with the advice and consent of the Senate, or by a Magistrate Judge, who is just as qualified but hired by the Court directly.

Magistrate Judges handle a lot of Social Security Disability cases, so they have specialized knowledge and experience with the Social Security Disability process. Also, you can often get your case handled faster if you agree to have a Magistrate Judge decide it. There is really no downside because you will never see this person anyway. You will never need to enter a courtroom. Everything will be done in writing.

The District Judge or Magistrate Judge will review the hearing transcript, the entire medical record, the ALJ decision, and any Appeals Council information. The Judge will also review arguments from your attorney and from the attorney representing the United States Government. That's right, you just sued the United States of America, and Uncle Sam needs to be represented as well. The Judge will then decide the legal issues in the case. There will not be a trial, there is no jury, and no one will testify. The District Judge or Magistrate Judge is simply deciding if the final decision of the Commissioner of Social Security (the ALJ decision or the Appeals Council decision) is supported by substantial evidence, or whether there are significant errors of law. These are the same issues that the Appeals Council already considered.

So, what is different about this appeal? The Federal Judge may decide that in fact there was not substantial evidence to support the decision, or the Judge may identify an error of law and disagree with the Appeals Council about its *significance*. The government attorney's job is to defend the final decision of the Commissioner of Social Security. That person is trying to convince the Judge to leave the SSA decision alone. But the District Judge or Magistrate Judge can really do whatever they want. As a result, a substantial number of cases are remanded back to SSA each year with instructions to redo something, even though the Appeals Council felt it was not a significant problem.

Whoever is presiding over the case at Federal Court will issue a written decision, which will have one of three outcomes. First, a finding in favor of SSA, which means the case is, in most situations, over. Theoretically, you could appeal to the United States Circuit Court of Appeals, but such action is pretty rare unless the representative has a specific legal issue they want that appellate court to resolve. Appeals take time and money, and it is unlikely that you would find a representative who would be willing to continue the case to the Court of Appeals or the United States Supreme Court.

The second possible outcome is a finding in favor of the claimant and a remand back to SSA, with instructions to give the claimant a new hearing and a new ALJ decision. This is the most common way for the claimant to win in Federal Court. Finally, in rare circumstances, the Federal Court could just order SSA to issue an approval of benefits, although this is problematic because if an error is identified, SSA likes to have an opportunity to correct that error. Some specific District Courts prefer this approach, but most would rather just send the case back to SSA. If the presiding Judge is a Magistrate Judge, that person will issue a recommended decision, and the supervising District Judge will approve it.

If your case goes back to an ALJ for a new hearing, you will start the process all over again from that stage. If you need to appeal again, the same process is followed, except you can skip the Appeals Council the second time around and go directly to Federal Court if you want. Hopefully this does not happen. If it does the process can

146

go on for years. The best way to avoid all of this is to make sure that your case has sufficient evidence, and also the right evidence to prove what you are trying to prove. Building a medical record starts well before you file your application for benefits. You need to make sure you are seeing the right medical sources, getting the right medical treatment, and that all of your treatment is well documented.

PART 4: What's the Best Evidence for Your Impairment?

21. Discussing Medical Evidence from a Lawyer's Perspective

I am not a doctor, and I do not profess to know anything in the medical world beyond what my SSA trainings have taught me. This chapter is NOT medical advice. I cannot stress that enough. This chapter is not legal advice either, since that can only come from a qualified representative who knows your specific situation. Like the rest of this book, this chapter offers general information, from my personal experience writing and reviewing thousands of Social Security Disability decisions, about what types of evidence SSA attorneys, Judges, and Appeals Officers generally look for when they see that a claimant is alleging inability to work due to a particular impairment or impairments.

Again, as I say throughout this book, this is not intended to be a DIY guide. There are plenty of other resources out there if that is the route you wish to go. As you know by now, I highly recommend against that. Once you finish this book, you will have a thorough understanding of how the Social Security Disability process works, including all the behind the scenes stuff SSA does not want you to know. But that does not mean you are qualified to represent yourself. You don't know the regulations, and you don't know how SSA will view your evidence. So please, *hire a representative* and talk to that person about your specific circumstances. That person will help you to get the precise evidence you need to prove your specific case and get the benefits you have earned.

Alright, I will step down off my soap box now so we can get to the evidence. I will break up this section into four categories. This might surprise people who think, "Well, there are physical impairments, like a back issue, and there are mental health impairments, like depression. What else could there be?" I am glad you asked! Below is the layout for the next four chapters. Again, this is just my own personal opinion of the best way to present this information. There is nothing official in my classification. It's the best way I can think to describe the different types of impairments that I have seen over the course of my Social Security career. Even so, there are frequently overlaps between these categories, since there is a wide range of how medical conditions impact people.

I will begin by discussing visible physical impairments. A common example in this category is a back disorder, such as lumbar disc degeneration. Second, I will discuss non-visible physical impairments. A common example in this category is a heart condition. Third, I will discuss mental health conditions with the potential for symptom management and improvement. These are impairments that *might*, with appropriate treatment, be considered as *potentially* not lifelong impairments. I am not suggesting these impairments are necessarily short term, just that they are capable in many circumstances of being treated with medication, therapy, counseling, etc. Common examples in this category are anxiety and depression. Finally, I will discuss mental health impairments that are generally considered to be permanent, including intellectual disorder, neurocognitive disorder, and autism spectrum disorder.

The final chapter in this section discusses how SSA treats the use of drugs and alcohol. Congress has said that if the reason you cannot work is primarily due to the use of drugs and/or alcohol, you cannot get disability benefits. This does not mean that everyone who occasionally has a beer or sometimes uses cannabis will be excluded. Many claimants have, at some point during their alleged period of disability, used alcohol in one form or another, or used some type of

150

unlawful substance (including cannabis, which remains a banned substance under the federal law). As a result, it will be necessary to explain to you how SSA treats the use of drugs and alcohol at the same time a person is alleging disability.

22. Visible Physical Impairments

First, let's look at visible physical impairments. These are impairments that a doctor can observe, either with the naked eye or on an imaging study. Before I started with Social Security, I had the same visual picture of someone who is disabled that many people likely have. For most of us, the only experience we have with that word is the blue and white icon we see on signs in parking lots across the United States. So, for many of us, a disabled person is someone who uses a wheelchair. But of course, that is not at all necessary for someone to meet Social Security's definition of disability, which focuses on medical impairments and how they impact a person's ability to work.

An example in this category is a back disorder, such as lumbar disc degeneration. Back disorder is, in fact, the most common impairment across all Social Security Disability claims. Other common impairments include bone fractures, knee degeneration, shoulder degeneration, and carpel tunnel syndrome. These impairments, which involve wear and tear of lumbar discs, ligaments, tendons, and joints are incredibly common, particularly among blue collar workers who have been doing physical jobs for many years.

Often, we find that these claimants started working at age 18 or earlier. So, by the time they get to age 48, they have been working 40 to 50 hours per week (sometimes more) for 30 years. Those jobs involve a lot of standing, walking, lifting, carrying, and bending, and all of that physical stress wears the body out. When we think of a 30 year career for someone like a police officer or a teacher, we think retirement with a pension. But for a construction laborer, plumber, warehouse worker, or even a retail store worker, what we actually find is someone who is not yet 50, likely does not have a college degree, and whose body carries a lifetime full of wear and tear that leaves the person unable to continue in that industry.

I cannot tell you how many cases I saw during my career where the claimant was 47 to 50 years of age. The profile I laid out in the previous paragraph is incredibly common, and I do not see this changing anytime in the next few decades so long as the education and labor system in the United States remains the same. A high school education is not worth what it was in the 1950s. When a person goes from high school directly into the workforce because that person does not want to go to college, cannot afford college, or just wants to or needs to starting earning money immediately to support a family, that decision can have a lifelong impact on the person's earning potential. That decision may also result in a gradual deterioration of the person's body during the ensuing decades. It is highly unlikely that person will make it from age 18 all the way to age 65 without experiencing some sort of major medical event that will prevent the person from being able to work.

Alright, enough bad news. Now let's turn to what a person with these types of impairments can do to show proof of their severity. The age of the claimant is not as relevant as showing why the impairments limit that person's ability to do full time work. I call these impairments "visible" because you can see someone limping, using crutches, using a cane, using a wheelchair, or wearing some sort of brace or wrap indicating that a physical impairment exists. Also, even if the impairment is not visible to the naked eye, a doctor would be able to see evidence of the impairment on an imaging study. I discuss visible physical impairments first because this is what people think of when they hear the word *disability*, but also because these impairments are the easiest to prove due to their objective nature.

Common examples of evidence for this category include x-rays, magnetic resonance imaging (MRI) studies, computerized tomography (CT) scans, ultrasound, and physical therapy reports with strength and/or extension testing (also known as "range of motion" testing). Treating or examining providers can see the impact of these impairments very clearly, so it is easier to determine the extent to which these impairments affect the claimant's ability to do physical activities.

If an injury occurred at work, which is common with warehouse jobs, for example, the claimant will have likely been evaluated by independent doctors who are occupational injury experts. These doctors know the precise way to evaluate whether an injury is work related, whether treatment would help, and when the person has reached maximum medical improvement. This is important evidence. If treatment is recommended, the Judge wants to see that the person was obtaining that specific treatment, such as physical therapy, in an effort to regain full use of the injured part of the body, thus making a return to work more likely.

While treatment is often expensive and cost prohibitive, some places are more affordable. The worst option is always the Emergency Department of a hospital, also called the Emergency Room, or ER. This is a place you should go if you are in a life threatening situation, as ER staff are highly trained at saving lives. But be aware that the ER is always the most expensive option for treatment. So, if you are in a life-or-death situation, and cost is a secondary concern, go to the ER. Otherwise, don't. There are cheaper and better alternatives.

If the initial injury was the result of a sudden incident, such as a car accident or an industrial injury (like something heavy falling on someone in a warehouse), the record may include an ER visit. However, ongoing treatment is often done with an outpatient provider because they are cheaper and easier to get to. Similarly, while you may need to see an orthopedist or a surgeon, good treatment can also be found with physical therapists, who are often qualified to conduct testing to determine your physical capabilities.

Some people choose chiropractic care, massage therapy, acupuncture, etc., for their treatment needs. These types of care are extremely helpful for many people. They help to ease pain caused by chronic conditions, whether they be injury-related or non-visible conditions like those I will discuss in Chapter 23. However, when it comes to how Social Security views this evidence, these alternative forms of care are less helpful as evidence.

In my experience, chiropractors will often exaggerate the physical limitations of their patients, making their reports seem unreliable. This is particularly true with car accident patients. In many cases, those appointments are being paid for by the medical portion of auto insurance. As a result, the chiropractor will often feel the need to justify substantial treatment, which means discussing the person's condition as if the person can barely walk. I don't know if it's simply a habit, but many times chiropractors will take this same approach when discussing other cases as well, even when there is not an auto insurance claim that needs to be justified. The result is that ALJs will not find chiropractic reports persuasive unless there is corroborating evidence elsewhere in the record.

Also, Social Security has very specific regulations regarding who is considered a "medical source" and who is not. This is another reason that Judges view the reports from chiropractors, massage therapists, acupuncturists, etc., as less reliable evidence of the claimant's physical limitations and capabilities, even though the actual care they provide is, many times, more valuable for the treatment and recovery of the person's condition than a visit to a surgeon's office.

A medical doctor may spend five minutes with a patient and never actually touch the person, making decisions after a short discussion and a review of the bloodwork or x-ray. Still, that medical doctor is considered a more authoritative source by the Judge. This is illogical, but this is how things are. In the United States, we just trust doctors more. That is starting to change as people are finding more affordable care with nurse practitioners, physician assistants, physical therapists, and naturopathic doctors, but old habits remain, and Judges like to see opinions from people who attended medical school.

I am not saying you should avoid these alternative forms of treatment if they help you feel better and be healthier. However, for your Social Security Disability claim, you will need more than alternative treatments. Chiropractic care, massage therapy, and acupuncture are wonderful treatment methods, but you should use these treatment methods for their health benefits, not for the potential evidence. That piece of paper (if your practitioner documents your sessions, and some may not), will not help much in your Social Security Disability case. That said, it is always best to get records from all treating sources, so make sure your alternative practitioners are keeping good records.

Still, in addition to alternative treatment methods, you will need objective testing, and you will need to show that you are seeking care with a medical doctor. There are pain management doctors who specialize in prescribing pain medication, but there are

156

also plenty of doctors out there that specialize in other methods of treatment. You just need to find what works best for you, and do what you can to treat the condition as effectively as possible. Your goal should be to try and get back to work, if possible. The Judge will know if you are genuinely seeking treatment, or just trying to build a paper trail for your disability claim. You won't fool the Judge, you have to actually seek care and try your best to improve your condition, or your claim is unlikely to be approved.

23. Non-Visible Physical Impairments

Next, let's review non-visible physical impairments. Chiropractors, massage therapists, and acupuncturists can also be tremendously helpful in treating these types of conditions. Common conditions in this category include diabetes, fibromyalgia, migraine headache, lupus, gout, Human Immunodeficiency Virus (HIV), cancer, neurological conditions like seizure disorder, and connective tissue disorders such as Ehlers-Danlos Syndrome (EDS). Other conditions in this category also include heart conditions, lung disease, liver disease, plantar fasciitis, and arthritis. Whether the person's condition is "visible" or "non-visible" largely depends on how the specific person is impacted.

For example, many people live with diabetes and no one knows, but if you have a severe case of diabetes, you may need to have a foot amputated or your eyesight may decline to the point of becoming vision-impaired. If you are impacted to the point of a visible limitation, consider the condition to be in the first category along with shoulder, knee, and back impairments. Similarly, if you have a mild back impairment, you may in fact be in this second category of non-visible impairments. It's all a matter of degree. For now, however, I will continue by discussing impairments that are not distinguishable by sight. In other words, when you look at the claimant, you would never know the person is suffering from a debilitating medical impairment.

Non-visible impairments can be more difficult to prove with evidence, but not always. For example, when it comes to cancer, CT scans and positron emission tomography (PET) scans are very useful in determining the degree of the condition. A heart condition can be diagnosed with a treadmill stress test or in a catheterization lab where instruments are inserted into the arteries to determine the degree of blockage. For diabetes, the key factor is the person's blood sugar, and how it moves up and down over time, and this can be easily tested as well. Lung disease can be measured with pulmonary function tests, and the degree of HIV advancement can be determined by looking at the person's white blood cell counts. So accurate objective testing is possible for some conditions in this category.

This is all good news for claimants, at least from the perspective of their disability claims, because it allows them to show the degree of the condition, which means a Judge can determine if it is improving or worsening over time. But there are some conditions, such as fibromyalgia, migraine headaches, and EDS, which cannot be easily measured. Often, persons with these conditions appear totally healthy, and they may be able to do some activities. It can be impossible to know just by looking at a person that their daily life is significantly disrupted and restricted. Because these conditions do not have good testing methods, they can be among the most difficult disability cases when it comes to convincing the Judge that you cannot do full time work.

Another condition that is very difficult to measure is seizure disorder. Because seizures happen at unpredictable times, often the only evidence will be descriptions of the seizure events from witnesses who are not medically trained. Sometimes the person will be wearing a seizure monitoring device at just the right time, so the best evidence can be captured and interpreted by a doctor, but this is rare. Usually, a seizure will happen at home, and the person's family will need to describe what they saw for a neurologist to be able to provide an accurate diagnosis.

For the other impairments noted above, evidence often comes solely in the form of symptoms. This is because many medical professionals do not know what objective evidence to obtain, meaning what tests or observations will show that these impairments have a significant impact on the person's ability to work.

This creates a real problem, because the SSA definition of disability requires clinical signs, symptoms, and laboratory findings. But many of these non-visible impairments have no clinical signs or laboratory findings to show that they exist. This is because, frankly, the medical community does not fully understand what causes seizures, migraine headaches, fibromyalgia pain, or connective tissue disorders. Some of these impairments are thought to have a genetic component, but it can often be difficult to obtain the required objective evidence.

For example, there are specific points on the body that may be tender for a person with fibromyalgia. When many of those tender points are noted all at the same time, the person is often diagnosed with fibromyalgia. But the problem for the Social Security Judge is that such a label does not explain what specific work related limitations that person has. The person may have fibromyalgia tender points and be found capable of medium work, or the Judge may decide that person cannot sustain a full time work schedule. Because tender point findings can be so widely interpreted, they are not particularly good evidence for a disability claim. Therefore, this claimant will need additional supporting evidence, such as observations or testing of the claimant's physical capabilities.

When a person with this sort of diagnostic label arrives at their hearing, and begins to testify, a lot of the statements tend to sound something like, "I just cannot work, I am in too much pain." I understand what this person is saying. I believe that almost everyone

160

who files for disability truly believes they are disabled. As I will address in Chapter 33, I do not think that "fraud, waste, and abuse" are a significant problem within the Social Security Disability system. There is just not enough money involved for fraud to occur.

Having said that, I do recognize that while claimants all believe they are disabled, the nationwide approval rate is around 50%. This means that while half of the people applying for disability benefits will be approved at some point in the process, this also means that half of all claimants will be denied throughout the process and end with no benefits. These people are in a lot of pain, they are tired all the time, and they feel they cannot sustain a full time work schedule.

Yet, because of the difficulty proving their impairments, their pain, and their fatigue, Social Security Judges tend to not believe these claimants. The Judges do not see the evidence they believe necessary to find these claimants disabled. They do not see evidence showing the claimant has pain or fatigue that is extreme enough to preclude a full time work schedule on a regular and continuing basis. It's sad, but this is how it is. Impairments in this category are difficult to prove, and as a result the approval rate tends to be lower than for claimants with visible physical impairments.

24. Mental Health Conditions with Potential Symptom Management

Now let's turn to the most common mental health impairments. These are mental health impairments that have the potential for symptom management under the right circumstances. Examples include: depressive disorder, anxiety disorder, personality disorder, bipolar disorder, eating disorder, somatoform disorder, trauma-related disorder, and even schizophrenia. Many people struggle their entire lives to get these impairments under control, and many times they are not successful. I am not saying that every person will receive effective treatment of these conditions, just that *sometimes* a person's symptoms can be managed successfully with appropriate treatment.

The evidence typically presented for impairments in this category include treatment notes from treating psychiatrists, psychologists, therapists, and counselors. Treating sources will discuss the claimant's symptoms, and also observations made during treatment sessions. Psychological testing may also be performed. SSA will also, just like with physical impairments, want the claimant to see a consultative examiner to determine what diagnoses are most appropriate, or possibly, to corroborate the findings and conclusions of the claimant's treating sources. The best thing I can say for these impairments is that it's very important to get consistent treatment. I recognize this can be difficult for someone who has depression, anxiety, or agoraphobia (fear of leaving your home). I further recognize this can be difficult for someone who likely does not have the financial means to get consistent treatment, which can be very expensive.

I understand that when you apply for Social Security Disability benefits, it's because you cannot work, which means you have minimal or no income. In the United States, where health insurance is typically linked with employment, this also means you likely have no private health insurance. Further, if you work part time, if your spouse has a job, or if you have even minimal assets, you may not qualify for Medicaid. In that situation, you may have no way to see medical sources affordably.

I get it, but many Judges do not. I cannot tell you how many times I have heard Judges (remember, the attorneys who write the decisions, which was my job, listen to the hearing recording after the hearing has concluded) ask a claimant, "Why didn't you get treatment?" And when the person cites a lack of funds, the Judge, who earns around $180,000 per year and has a federal employee healthcare plan, would then ask, "Well why didn't you just go to the Emergency Room?"

Such a question would always make me cringe. As I said earlier, the ER is a terrible place for the treatment of chronic mental health conditions such as depression, anxiety, or personality disorder. ER staff often outright refuse to treat these mental health conditions because they assume the person coming there for treatment is a drug seeker who just wants pills. Also, ER staff cannot do much for mental health patients other than write a prescription and recommend counseling or therapy. They cannot provide the ongoing services that most people need.

Further, this question fails to account for the fact that going to the Emergency Room is expensive *even if you have insurance*! Without insurance, the costs can be unfathomable. Even though you don't have to pay anything on the day of your visit, that doesn't mean it's free. An ER will treat a person who is dying regardless of

163

that person's ability to pay, but all uninsured patients in the United States get a bill after the fact, and those bills are often unpayable even with the Judge's salary. A person can negotiate a bill with a hospital, and there are also some charities that can help negotiate the cost of services or outright pay the bill for the patient. Still, due to the substantial cost of hospital treatment, for a chronic condition, the ER is not the best place to get the care you need.

Sometimes a Judge will also ask, "Well did you consider going to a free, reduced price, or walk-in clinic?" That is a better, but still condescending, question. I would not blame the claimant for thinking, "Hey Judge, don't you think if I could have found a place near my home, that I could afford, that would be able to help me, *I would have gone?*" Maybe the claimant could not find a clinic near their home, or could not get transportation, or still could not afford the *reduced* price. These are all reasonable situations for someone who is not working, has mobility issues, has mental health difficulties, and/or lives in a small town or rural area.

The bottom line is that it is often *extremely* difficult for claimants who have no money to get treatment, even if they have good transportation, access to treatment, know where to get it, and can get themselves to the appointments. Pile on top of all that a fear of other people, a fear of leaving one's home, feelings of anxiety or depression, and other metal health difficulties, and it is understandable why so many people find it a challenge to obtain regular treatment, especially for mental health impairments.

Also, even if they can establish and begin treatment, persons with mental health challenges often have difficulty remembering appointments, getting to appointments, paying attention during sessions, remembering to take medication, or do assigned exercises after the appointment. This is not a refusal to engage in treatment *for*

164

the impairment, it's a symptom *of* the impairment and should not be held against the claimant, yet it often is.

Having said all that, the Judge does need to see evidence to substantiate the impairment and to prove that the limitations the claimant alleges do indeed prevent the claimant from working. So, while treatment can be very expensive, a claimant does have to do something to show the Judge that the impairment exists, and that the person is making active efforts to reduce symptoms so that a return to work could be possible. Judges really like to see that a person asking for benefits is trying their best to not need benefits for too long. They strongly dislike a claimant alleging a treatable impairment but not making the effort to seek treatment, or not participating fully in treatment.

The point here is that if a mental health condition is the reason you cannot work, you need to try your best to do whatever you can to get whatever treatment you can to reduce your symptoms. Mental health professionals are not dumb, they can tell when you are trying and when you are simply giving them lip service. The same goes for Judges, who can tell by reading the mental health treatment reports and by speaking with you at the hearing whether you are serious about trying to reduce your mental health symptoms.

I understand this can be very difficult, but the effort is what really counts. Results are less important because Judges understand that not everyone has tremendous success, particularly if you are applying for disability benefits. They presume that unless you are saying you got better and went back to work (in which case you are seeking a closed period of disability), that you have not had significant improvement of your symptoms. But they want to know that you are trying. The worst thing you can do is lie to the Judge, lie to a treatment source who is trying to help you, or attend a treatment session when you do not have a desire for it to actually help reduce your symptoms.

If you show up to counseling or therapy with a "why am I here?" attitude, or worse, you indicate to the provider that you are only there to get documentation for your disability claim, the provider will explain all of that in the medical report. When the Judge reviews that report, the Judge will understand that you do not have any intention of trying to reduce your symptoms and go back to work, and your claim for benefits will be swiftly denied.

If you cannot afford mental health services, and if you do not have access to Medicaid, there may be lower cost alternatives in your area. You could look for a reduced price clinic, since many states and local governments offer treatment options for people with minimal or no income. You could also look for student clinics which you might find at a local university or community college. Perhaps your local area may even have private practices where the counselor has a master's degree instead of a Ph.D., which usually means they charge less for equally good services. Or maybe you could look for someone who will let you commit to sessions at a bulk rate. For example, if a normal rate is $80 per hour, but you commit to 10 counseling sessions, maybe you can get those 10 sessions for $500, or $50 per hour, even if you cannot pay in advance. Or, perhaps you can find a provider who will do 30 minute sessions instead of hour long sessions, which of course would be cheaper because you will only get half the time with the provider.

But perhaps the best kept secret (not so secret anymore thanks to the pandemic) is mental health treatment via telehealth. By using the internet, you can engage with a provider anywhere in the country, or at least anywhere in your state (some states only allow their licensed providers to provide service to clients within the state).

166

Telehealth visits tend to be cheaper, and they are always more convenient. They are an excellent option for mental health treatment because, unlike with physical impairments, the provider does not need to physically touch the patient. It's just a conversation, done by video over the internet or by using an app on your phone. Sometimes, these appointments are very low cost, or even free with a nurse.

Many employers also have Employee Assistance Programs (EAP), so if you have a part time job, you could consider that resource as well. Also, remember that if your spouse, parent, or child has access to any of these programs, you may also be able to access them and obtain the services you need. Get creative, as you may be eligible for certain free or low cost services and not yet know it. The bottom line is, you should do anything you can to get your impairment diagnosed, and then you should pursue whatever treatment you can find and afford, even if you think you may never be able to work full time in the future. Before starting with any provider, make sure you will be able to get good documentation for your sessions so you can show the Judge you are trying every way possible to obtain treatment for your symptoms.

25. Permanent Mental Health Conditions

Now let's turn to permanent mental health conditions. Examples include: intellectual disorder, neurocognitive disorder, and autism spectrum disorder. While you may not think of impairments in this category as mental impairments, they are categorized as mental disorders by the DSM-V and by SSA regulations. Therefore, SSA Judges view these conditions as mental impairments. Still, I acknowledge they are different from the impairments in the previous category because, even with treatment, these conditions are permanent. Treatment will not result in any substantial degree of improvement.

For the first impairment, "intellectual disorder" is the term outlined in the Diagnostic and Statistical Manual of Mental Disorders, Fifth Edition (DSM-V), revised in 2013 and again in 2022. The full criteria for intellectual disorder are laid out at Listing 12.05. The listing requires evidence of significantly subaverage general intellectual functioning, evidence of significant deficits in adaptive functioning (meaning the person depends upon others for basic personal needs), and evidence that the disorder began prior to age 22.

To show significantly subaverage general intellectual functioning, there must be evidence of an IQ score below a certain level. When a person undergoes an IQ test, three scores are reported: full scale, verbal, and performance. The regulations allow for consideration of the lowest of the three reported scores, which helps claimants who have a more pronounced deficit in one area of functioning.

As flawed as IQ testing may be, the IQ test is still considered to be the best evidence for this criterion. Because IQ scores typically do not change throughout a person's life, testing done at different times should produce similar test results. Therefore, an IQ score within the regulatory range, regardless of when the testing was done, is considered to also be evidence of onset of the impairment before age 22.

A person can be found to have this condition, and can even be found disabled by a Judge, but this does not mean that the person will never be able to work! Many people with intellectual disorder can do simple, repetitive tasks, where expectations can be clearly explained and understood. An excellent example of such work is a grocery bagger. My local grocery store employs a person with intellectual disorder. He is the hardest working employee in the store, and customers love him.

A person can work part time, earn less than the SGA amount, and continue to receive benefits, and that is perfectly lawful and within SSA regulations. Or, the person may want to work full time, which would mean earning at the SGA level. This, of course, means the Social Security Disability benefits would stop, but often persons with intellectual disorder find work to be an important and valuable experience. It gives some people a sense of belonging and confidence, and helps them to feel like they can be just as productive as everyone else.

I do need to address the concept of supportive work environments (also called sheltered work), which do not count as SGA. Above, I described a person who has intellectual disorder but who can work as a grocery bagger under the same expectations and standards of conduct as other employees. He is treated the same as every other store employee, and he is really good at his job. But there are some work environments where the person is paid the same as a non-impaired employee even though the work is done at a slower pace, or is of less quality than that of a non-impaired employee. Think of a supportive work environment as a place for a person with intellectual disorder to go to learn how to do a job, and to get paid while learning. In a supportive work environment, because the person is learning, there are no penalties for misbehavior, for failing to do the job at an adequate pace, and for not fully serving the customer.

Here is an example of a supportive work environment. In a grocery store setting, imagine a person with intellectual disorder being taught how to bag groceries. The bread comes down the conveyor belt first and the worker places the bread into the bag. Then comes a watermelon, so he grabs it and begins to place it into the bag. Standing next to that person is another store employee who intercepts the watermelon and places it *under* the loaf of bread, so it does not squish the bread. This is a way of teaching the person on the job while he is being paid, while being supportive and tolerant of mistakes that might get a non-impaired employee fired.

The person with intellectual disorder is being given an opportunity to learn how to do the work in an environment where mistakes are expected, tolerated, and taught through, even if they are repetitive. Any money earned in such an environment is not considered SGA, and will therefore not prevent the person from being found disabled to begin with or from continuing to receive benefits. The work is only considered "gainful" once it is being done at the same standard as a non-impaired employee. Some persons with intellectual disorder, neurocognitive disorder, and autism spectrum disorder get to that point, but others may only be able to participate in supportive work.

Here is another question you may have already thought of: How can someone who has never been able to work full time

170

possibly earn Social Security quarter credits to become insured and therefore qualify for Title 2 benefits? Does that person only qualify for Title 16? The answer is the person can qualify for both, but there are very specific requirements. I have already explained the strict income and asset qualifications for Title 16, and all of those would apply to a person with intellectual disorder. Since many people with intellectual disorder do not live on their own, that person perhaps lives with a family member, and the "free rent" may then reduce the person's SSI benefits. For this reason, it's important to know how that person can access Title 2 benefits instead.

The rest of this explanation assumes the person has not worked long enough to earn their own Social Security credits sufficient to become fully insured and have insured status. If that has happened, the person could file a claim on their own Social Security record. But if not, there is an alternative. There is a unique part of the law that allows someone to apply for and collect Title 2 benefits on someone else's account. The person can have any impairment, but it certainly seems to me that this part of the law was specifically designed with intellectual disorder in mind.

Here is how it works. First, because this is a Title 2 claim, the claimant must be an adult. Since the person does not have their own insured status, the person can file a Title 2 claim on someone else's Social Security record. Typically, for a person age 18 to 22, this means the person's parent. SSA employees refer to this type of claimant as a "disabled adult child," because the person is an adult, but is the child of the record holder. This claim is therefore referred to within SSA as a "DAC" claim. One challenge though is that the record holder (the parent) must be dead, disabled, or retired. Only then can the "disabled adult child" collect Title 2 benefits on the parent's account.

If the parent is not dead, disabled, or retired while the claimant is age 18 to 22, the claimant can file a Title 2 claim later, even much later. As I indicated, the IQ test is itself proof that the person developed intellectual disorder before age 22. So, when the claimant is 30, or 35, or even 40, and a parent dies, is found disabled, or files a retirement claim, at that point the "disabled adult child" can file a Title 2 disability claim, even though that person is well beyond age 22.

Now let's turn to the next impairment: neurocognitive disorder. This condition is different because it's not a condition a person is born with. The criteria for this impairment are laid out at Listing 12.02, which requires evidence of a "significant cognitive decline from a prior level of functioning." Here is an example to illustrate what this means: An orthopedic surgeon who has several college degrees and certifications is involved in a car accident, after which he regains some cognitive ability. However, an IQ test shows similar results to someone with intellectual disorder. This is evidence of a significant cognitive decline from the doctor's prior level of functioning due to a traumatic brain injury (TBI).

Think of the difference between intellectual disorder and neurocognitive disorder this way. A claimant with intellectual disorder and a claimant with neurocognitive disorder may have similar IQ test results. The difference is whether there was a significant cognitive decline during the person's life. With neurocognitive disorder, the cognitive decline could be due to a sudden, traumatic event such as a car accident, a fall, or even a substance overdose. Or, the cognitive decline could happen more slowly, as is the case with dementia.

For evidence of the person's functioning prior to the cognitive decline, SSA will consult descriptions from friends,

172

family, supervisors, co-workers, etc., describing the person's life prior to the decline. The Judge will evaluate whether the new and significantly reduced degree of intellectual functioning would allow the person to sustain a full time work schedule on a regular and continuing basis. If the person was capable of working before, and now is not, the person would likely be found disabled. This is the case even if the situation was caused by a substance overdose. I will explain why that is the case in Chapter 26.

One final note about neurocognitive disorder. Let's return briefly to the orthopedic surgeon example above. The work that person used to do is as skilled and specialized as it gets. There is no doubt the person will no longer be able to do that work after suffering a TBI. But notice I did not say the claimant needs to be able to return to the same work that was done before the traumatic event. This claimant is evaluated the same as every other Social Security Disability claimant. At Step 5 of the sequential evaluation process, the question is whether the person can do any other full time work that exists in significant numbers in the national economy. So, when the Judge evaluates the new and significantly reduced degree of intellectual functioning, the Judge only needs to decide whether that person can do simple, repetitive, unskilled work, such as the grocery bagger job. If that work can be done on a full time basis, the person will be found not disabled.

The final impairment in this section is autism spectrum disorder. The criteria for this condition, as laid out in SSA regulations at Listing 12.10, require medical documentation of qualitative deficits in verbal communication, nonverbal communication, and social interaction. The criteria also require evidence of significantly restricted, repetitive patterns of behavior, interests, or activities. The evidence is typically observational in nature and may include psychological evaluations, treatment notes, and evaluations from physical, occupational, and speech therapists.

The criteria for all three impairments in this chapter is very specific. As a result, many Judges will call a medical expert to appear at the hearing to evaluate the claimant's medical record. The medical expert will then testify whether, in their opinion, the claimant's condition meets the strict requirements of the applicable listing. The medical expert may also provide testimony as to whether the person's impairment is *medically equivalent* to the severity described by a specific listing. Finally, the medical expert may state an opinion as to whether the person could perform full time work on a regular and continuing basis.

26. Drug Abuse and Alcoholism (DAA)

SSA refers to issues surrounding substance abuse by the somewhat old-fashioned term "drug abuse and alcoholism" which is often referenced simply by its abbreviation, DAA. I note that a person does not need to necessarily be abusing drugs, or be considered an alcoholic. This is simply a phrase from a law passed in 1996 (Public Law 104-121) that says SSA will not pay someone benefits if drug or alcohol use is causing the claimant to be unable to work. However, not all drug or alcohol use disqualifies a person from benefits. It all depends on what, specifically, is causing the claimant to be unable to work.

If the claimant's impairments, not including drug abuse or alcoholism, would result in a finding that the claimant is disabled, then the claimant is disabled. However, if, when drug abuse or alcoholism are removed from consideration, the remainder of the claimant's impairments would *not* result in a finding that the claimant is disabled, then the claimant is *not* disabled. The reason is that in such a circumstance, it is the drug or alcohol use that *caused* the claimant to be disabled. SSA makes this determination by performing two sequential evaluation analyses.

First, the Judge will analyze *all* of the impairments in the record, including any drug or alcohol use impairments. Yes, that's right, drug and alcohol use are considered to be medical impairments. Many times, these impairments will appear in mental health treatment or Emergency Department records. For example, if a person is regularly falling down and injuring his shoulder, but each time the ER performs toxicology screening which shows the claimant was using alcohol, there are actually two impairments: a physical shoulder injury and substance use disorder. But what we do not yet know is whether the non-substance impairment would be sufficient on its own to find the claimant disabled.

The same analysis is done for mental health impairments. If a person is noted to have numerous suicide attempts, there will likely be a diagnosis of depression with suicidal ideation. This is one impairment. But if the ER records also indicate the claimant was using heroin, this will also be considered during the first sequential evaluation analysis, since substance abuse is considered to be a separate impairment.

During the first sequential evaluation, all of the claimant's impairments are taken into account, including all substance use impairments. If, after doing that analysis, it is determined that the claimant can do past relevant work (Step 4) or other work that exists in significant numbers in the national economy (Step 5), the Judge will simply find the claimant not disabled and the analysis will end. Since the claimant is found able to work, there is no need for a second sequential evaluation analysis to determine if substance abuse is causing the claimant to be *unable* to work. The second sequential evaluation analysis is only done if the claimant is found disabled with the substance impairments factored in.

If, after the first sequential evaluation analysis, it is determined that a person engaging in drug or alcohol use would be disabled (at either Step 3 or Step 5), then the law requires the Judge to perform a second sequential evaluation analysis. However, this time, the drug and/or alcohol use will be removed from consideration, and only the other impairments will be considered. In the examples above, this means the shoulder impairment or the depressive disorder. If, during that second sequential evaluation analysis, the Judge determines the person can do past relevant work

(Step 4) or other work that exists in significant numbers in the national economy (Step 5), the person will be found not disabled.

The only difference between the first and second sequential evaluation analysis is the removal of the substance use disorder from consideration. Since doing so caused the outcome to change from disabled to not disabled, substance use must be what caused the claimant to be found disabled during the first evaluation. In such a circumstance, the law does not allow that person to receive Social Security Disability benefits. Accordingly, the second sequential evaluation analysis will prevail, and the claimant will be found not disabled.

The reason for doing the sequential evaluation process twice is that Congress has decided that benefits should not be paid if a person is causing a state of disability by using drugs or alcohol. In such a circumstance, the person will not be able to get disability benefits even though the person cannot work. The person will not be able to get benefits even though the substance abuse addiction is just that, an addiction, for which people require treatment, and from which it is extremely difficult to escape. But that's the law until Congress decides otherwise.

However, not everyone who uses drugs and/or alcohol will be denied benefits. Taking the examples above, if the shoulder injury is so bad the person cannot use the arm to do even sedentary work (which involves significant use of the arms and hands, like for typing), and perhaps is in so much pain that he cannot sustain a full time work schedule, then the person would be found disabled during that second sequential evaluation when the alcohol use is removed from consideration. In that case, the person is found disabled solely based on the severity of the shoulder impairment.

In the other example, if the person, without the heroin use considered, is still having such significant depression with suicidal ideation that she could not tolerate supervision, being around others, or the demands of a full time work schedule, then that person would be found disabled even when the heroin use is removed from consideration. Thus, in both cases, even though the person is using alcohol or drugs, substance use is not the *reason* the person is disabled. Accordingly, the Judge would still find each of those persons to be disabled under SSA regulations.

Now let's explore what substances are considered to be "drugs" for the purpose of a Social Security Disability claim. SSA Judges treat prescription drugs differently from other drugs. If use of a substance is not illegal, Social Security Judges tend to see abuse of that drug as less bad. This is odd, since opiate drugs like oxycodone have essentially the same chemical makeup as heroin. Congress deems the injected form to be illegal, but the far more expensive pill form (sold by large pharmaceutical companies with a lot of lobbying power) to be legal. This matters to a lot of Judges.

However, this distinction between legal and illegal is somewhat blurred when it comes to cannabis. This is a substance that has been legalized at the state level as a medicinal substance for over 25 years (the first state was California, in 1996). Since then, not only have a majority of states adopted at least legal medical cannabis, but many have opted to eliminate the need for a prescription. Instead, many states now have so-called *recreational* cannabis, which means people over the age of consent, usually 21, can walk into a state-regulated cannabis store and purchase it.

I do not like the term "recreational" because it suggests that everyone is now "smoking weed" just for fun. In fact, many people across the country use cannabis for medicinal reasons, without

178

having to get a prescription first. We don't say "recreational aspirin," we just say "over-the-counter," and that's what we have in many states, over-the-counter cannabis. Colorado and Washington were the first two states to implement this system, but voters and legislatures in many other states have opted to skip the need for a prescription with this over-the-counter approach.

Again, I note I am not a doctor or psychologist, but from many years of experience reading medical documents, I know that cannabis is used to treat a wide variety of medical and psychological impairments. Cannabis can help reduce symptoms from physical ailments, such as back, knee, and shoulder issues, as well as migraine headaches, lupus, fibromyalgia, and the effects of diabetes. Also, people with heart conditions, cancer, or other mobility-restricting issues may use cannabis, and often notice positive results. Cannabis can also be used for mental health difficulties, such as depression, anxiety, suicidal ideation, personality disorder, etc. Often, cannabis helps where more traditional treatments, like opioid medications or surgery, fail to provide adequate relief.

However, while many states recognize that it no longer makes sense to deem cannabis illegal, the United States Congress has not yet reached that point. So, we have this very strange scenario where a person can be legally purchasing, possessing, and using cannabis products in their state, but once they admit to doing so in a federal administrative procedure, they are acknowledging a serious violation of federal law.

Luckily, the Administrative Law Judges I have spoken to over the years acknowledge that difference in the law. Many Judges seem to understand that many people are using cannabis to treat or cope with pain or mental health difficulties. Most Judges also understand that cannabis is seldom the reason a person cannot work.

They understand that most people who are using cannabis and applying for disability benefits are using cannabis to treat their symptoms. As a result, most Judges would be unlikely to find that cannabis use is the disabling factor that causes the claimant to be unable to work.

These Judges deserve some credit. As I said, cannabis is a substance that is banned under federal law. Still, Social Security Judges are not living under a rock. They understand that people use cannabis, and that many times it provides a noticeable medical benefit, even if the person still is not able to work. This is especially true in states where there is a legal structure for the cultivation, distribution, sale, purchase, and use of cannabis products. Judges in these states see a lot of people who use cannabis, and in many cases, they appreciate that the claimant is trying to improve and return to work.

Throughout the last few paragraphs, I have been using the term "cannabis" to describe the consumable part of the cannabinoid plant. I prefer this term because it comes from the latin name for the plant itself. However, many Judges will use the more old-fashioned term, "marijuana." Common use of that term began in the 1930s as a way to link use of this plant and its medicinal properties with its use by Mexican immigrants to the United States. The term was used to demonize not only use of the plant, but more specifically the people who were using it. Almost 100 years later, I see no reason to continue along that path. However, many Social Security Judges will still use that term, possibly not understanding its prejudicial origin.

This is one way you can tell whether your Judge tends to be more hostile towards people who use cannabis. In my experience, if your Judge uses the term "cannabis," the Judge will likely be tolerant of your use. On the other hand, if you encounter a Judge who asks you if you have ever used "marijuana," you should not lie, but you should be prepared for that Judge to make a big deal out of such use. That Judge may suggest that you are using a very serious, illegal drug.

You may even be in the unfortunate situation of appearing in front of a Judge who never, or almost never, approves any cases where the claimant is using (or has ever used) drugs or alcohol. Such action is, of course, completely prejudicial and inappropriate, but you should know these Judges do exist. Their attitude tends to be, "You're not getting my tax dollars to go out and buy drugs or booze." And as for the legal aspect of their action, their attitude is, "You don't like my decision? Appeal."

You may be assigned this kind of Judge. For all the reasons I provide throughout this book, from the hiring process to the way that Judges are reviewed and evaluated, many Judges are biased in this way. If this happens, you can file a complaint against a Judge if you feel bias played a part in the decision, and someone will look at your complaint. I do not know the specifics of that procedure, but I do know two things. First, the bias complaint will not get looked at until after your case has a final resolution. This does not mean that your claim of a biased Judge will be ignored. The Appeals Council or a Federal Court could reverse the decision if you can prove bias, but the bias complaint against that specific ALJ is set aside until after your case has concluded.

Second, that bias complaint needs to have *very* strong support. Bias claims are reviewed on an "abuse of discretion" standard, meaning you have to prove the Judge abused their authority. You cannot allege bias because you disagree with the decision, or with some aspect over which the Judge had discretion. For example, if the Judge decides to accept one medical opinion over another, and provides supporting rationale, you cannot say that the Judge was biased against you. The Judge has the authority to make that call. A bias complaint can only be lodged when the Judge does not have the authority to do something but does it anyway. For example, if the Judge denies your claim because you once used cannabis long before you allege disability began, this is not how the DAA rule works, so you could allege bias. The problem is that a bias claim is very difficult to prove because a smart Judge, albeit a biased one, can easily disguise such bias by providing some rational basis for the decision.

For example, even if you are sure that your cannabis use is the reason the Judge denied your claim, all the Judge has to do is talk about how you did not get enough treatment, or how one time you did not follow medical advice. In other words, all the Judge has to do is provide *any* rationale that diverts attention from what you suspect to be the real reason for the denial, and the Judge will likely be cleared of bias.

There is something else you need to know about accusing a Judge of bias. A bias claim will never result in anything beneficial for you. All that would happen is that the Judge would be disciplined. Bias allegations are reviewed after your case is over because they basically do not involve you. So, for your disability claim, the best thing to do is not to focus on a bias complaint, but to bring up the suspected bias as an issue on appeal. Such appeals are often successful and result in a new hearing.

Normally, an ALJ can hear a case twice before being removed from the case. This is because SSA likes to give a Judge one chance to correct any errors that occurred the first time around. However, if you claim bias during the appeal, and if the case is remanded to the hearing level for a new hearing for that reason, then

182

the case will not go back to the same Judge even a second time. If bias is involved, the Appeals Council will direct that the case be sent to a different Judge for your new hearing. Note that I said nothing about whether this will be a *better* Judge, just a *different* Judge. This person could be more biased, you never know.

Something else to keep in mind about the use of drugs and/or alcohol, is that such use is often linked to one very specific physical impairment: liver disease. The most common situation is that a person has an alcohol addiction that results in hepatitis, and after many years, ends up resulting in cirrhosis of the liver. At that point, the person may become so ill that the person cannot sustain a full time work schedule on an ongoing basis. And because cirrhosis is irreversible, the inability to work is likely permanent unless the person could obtain a liver transplant, which is unlikely for a person with such a significant history of alcohol use. Since the claimant destroyed their liver through a long history of alcohol abuse, one would think there is no possible way the law allows that person to get disability benefits, right? Wrong.

This is an excellent scenario to demonstrate an SSA concept known as, "We take the claimant that comes before us." When I described the use of two sequential evaluations above for DAA cases, the second time around I explained that we remove the drug and/or alcohol use from consideration, and we analyze all of the other impairments to see if the claimant would remain disabled. In this case, the cirrhosis of the liver is so bad the person is still considered disabled as of the AOD, even if he continues to use alcohol after that date.

Stated another way, even if a person has destroyed their liver with decades of substance abuse, the analysis the Judge conducts does not factor any of that in. The ALJ can only consider the following question: If, during the period at issue in the case, the claimant had ceased use of drugs and/or alcohol, would the remaining impairments(s) still result in a finding of disability? In our example, the claimant's liver is destroyed, and this causes such significant symptoms that working a full time schedule is simply not possible. This would, of course, remain the case even if the person stopped using alcohol. Cirrhosis is a permanent and irreversible impairment. Once you destroy the liver, there is no way back. Another way to say this is, "What's done is done."

There are a lot of Judges who detest this policy, but they are required to follow it. It's the law. All the Judges can do is apply it, even if they don't like to. SSA takes the claimant's body, and all the impairments that are presented, as they are, and the only ones we can selectively ignore are the substance use impairments. Congress allows that. But Congress does not allow SSA to ignore the *result* of that long period of substance use, which in this case is the resulting liver disease. Therefore, a person in this situation would be found disabled even though that person's actions *caused* the very impairment which results in the finding of disability.

Another similar situation is a drug overdose resulting in a traumatic brain injury (TBI). In such a situation, the fact that the claimant engaged in an action that caused the disabling situation is not relevant under the law. However, this example is a bit different. With the prior example, the person continued to use alcohol into the alleged period of disability. However, in a drug overdose TBI scenario, the person usually does not continue to use drugs. There is usually a single overdose event, which causes a TBI, and which therefore represents the AOD. However, after that event, the claimant typically does not continue to use substances.

184

Because the person has stopped using drugs as of the AOD, in this scenario there is no DAA issue to analyze at all. Remember, the person's past use of substances is not relevant. All that matters is use during the alleged period of disability. In this situation, there is no ongoing use. Thus, if, by the time the person alleges disability began, enough damage has been done to support a finding of disability, the person would likely be found disabled and awarded benefits.

If you are thinking, "Ah, so there is a way to guarantee myself benefits after all," all I can say is: No. End-stage cirrhosis or traumatic brain injury is not the way to go. The former means you are close to death, and in a lot of pain, with no way out, and the latter means your brain injury is so severe you may need significant care for the rest of your life. Either way, you will require substantial financial support that costs way more than you will ever get in Social Security Disability benefits. These are horrible circumstances, so while the law does allow someone to destroy their brain or body and then get disability benefits, it's not worth doing intentionally. If you are dealing with a family member in this situation, Social Security will be there to help, but the help is minimal, and insufficient to care for that person's needs.

Finally, before we leave DAA, I need to address something which you may be thinking, something which I thought about when I first learned about the DAA rules. Drugs are bad, alcohol is bad, but what about cigarettes, aren't they bad too? Of course they are, but they are not included in the DAA law, and this is no accident.

When I asked about this during my initial SSA training, it was explained to me that when Congress put the law into place in 1996, they did so with a very specific intent to exclude cigarettes. Why? Tobacco is "a fine product of the south." There are a lot of members of Congress from the south, where tobacco is primarily grown. In the 1990s, it was still considered to be a fine product, and any alleged harmfulness had not yet been fully proven, at least as far as the tobacco companies were concerned. So, the law targeted cannabis, a competitor to cigarettes, while leaving cigarettes alone. As such, if you are using cigarettes, and by doing so you destroy your lungs to the point that you cannot work, you are eligible for benefits. And if you continue to use cigarettes right up until the hearing, there will still be no DAA analysis. There will be just one sequential evaluation. You are not using "drugs or alcohol" under the law.

Tobacco abuse is simply not considered in the same way as drug use or alcohol use. Does this mean that someone can smoke until the lungs are destroyed, get disability benefits, and then just keep on smoking? Yes. That person could also walk into the local Social Security office, cigarette in hand, and ask about the next benefits check. A person does not need to hide tobacco use, it is not considered DAA. However, some Judges will consider whether you followed the advice of your doctor. If you have a lung impairment, and you continue to smoke, the Judge could deny your claim because you refused to follow specific medical advice to stop smoking. But this is not a DAA finding, it's a finding that you did not follow your doctor's treatment recommendation.

Finally, I acknowledge that most people would not continue to smoke or use drugs or alcohol as I suggested above unless they are addicted and just cannot stop. Social Security Disability benefits are minimal, insufficient to pay all of life's regular bills, let alone medical bills for a terminal condition. Such benefits are not worth destroying the only body and mind you will ever have. So, if you think there are people out there "gaming the system" this way, you

186

can relax, that just isn't happening. In Chapter 33, I discuss the concept of "fraud, waste, and abuse," and why it's not the problem many people make it out to be.

PART 5: Uncommon Situations

27. Child Claimants, Deceased Claimants, and Widow Claimants

No one wants to think about disabled children, deceased claimants, or claimants who have lost their spouses, but these cases do happen. Let's start with child cases. Some child cases involve impairments since birth, while others involve impairments that start later in childhood. If the claimant is under the age of 18, the case will be SSI only, because the SSDI program is only for adults. If the case continues beyond age 18, SSDI can then be considered. But for children, SSI is the only option. The reason can be summarized with a three word phrase that I was taught during my SSA training: *kids don't work.*

Because SSDI involves credits earned through working, and because *kids don't work*, child claims can only be for SSI benefits. As with all Title 16 cases, there are income and asset limitations, and in those cases SSA considers the income and assets of the parent/guardian when determining if a child claimant is eligible for SSI. If benefits are paid because the child is found disabled, the parent/guardian receives the money as the "representative payee" to manage on the child's behalf.

You may remember "disabled adult child" cases from earlier in the book. Those are Title 2 cases where the claimant can apply for and receive benefits on someone else's earnings record (usually a parent), so long as that person is dead, disabled, or retired. But for those cases, the claimant must be an adult, and disability needs to be established between ages 18 and 22. So once the child turns 18, this type of claim is also a possibility, but not while the claimant is under the age of 18.

The most important difference between adult and child cases is the different sequential evaluation. Because *kids don't work*, the five-step sequential evaluation process does not apply. There cannot be an RFC, an analysis of past work, or an analysis of possible other work. Instead, the sequential evaluation process ends at Step 3. If a listed impairment is not met, and if the severity of the child's impairments does not medically equal a listed impairment, then the Judge will decide whether the listings, as a whole, are *functionally equaled*. In other words, is the child's functioning so bad that it is equivalent to a listed impairment?

To make this determination, the Judge will review six domains of childhood functioning: acquiring and using information; attending and completing tasks; interacting and relating with others; moving about and manipulating objects; caring for yourself; and health and physical wellbeing. The Judge will consult SSA guidance that provide specific capabilities a child should have depending on the child's age, and decide if the evidence shows a marked or extreme limitation in any of the six domains of functioning. If the Judge finds two marked limitations or one extreme limitation, the Judge will find the child claimant disabled.

This is a highly subjective finding, so for almost all child cases, the Judge will call a medical expert to testify at the hearing. The medical expert will assess the evidence in the medical record as it relates to the six domains of functioning. The medical expert will need to be either a pediatrician or an impairment specialist. So, if the child has a heart condition, the expert could be a cardiologist. For mental impairments, a mental health specialist, such as a psychologist or psychiatrist, would be necessary if a pediatrician is not available.

It is also difficult to imagine anyone passing away before a decision can be issued, but this does happen. The claimant must be alive at the time a claim is filed, but sometimes a claimant passes away while the claim is pending. For an SSDI claim, involving earned benefits, the Judge can still issue a decision in the case, with the benefits being paid to a "substitute party." These cases obviously involve a closed period of benefits, ending with the claimant's date of death. There will be no ongoing monthly benefits because someone who is deceased cannot collect Social Security benefits. But, the claimant's substitute party can be paid any past due benefits the claimant was entitled to receive while alive.

For SSDI claims, SSA allows a surviving spouse, a surviving child, a surviving parent, or the legal representative of the claimant's estate to be a substitute party. For most cases, there will be someone who fits at least one of these categories. For SSI cases, the requirements are more strict. For most SSI claims, the only person who can be a substitute party is a surviving spouse. If a child claimant dies, a parent/guardian can be a substitute party. A knowledgeable, qualified representative can tell you if you meet the strict eligibility criteria. If there is no qualifying substitute party, and if the claimant's state provided certain services while the person was alive (like state-funded healthcare), the state can stand in as a substitute party and collect the past due SSI benefits. If that did not occur, an SSI claim for a deceased claimant will simply be dismissed.

Finally, I would like to briefly introduce the concept of a Disabled Widow's Benefits (DWB) claim. For such a claim, you must be at least 50 years of age, and be a widow(er), meaning your spouse has passed away. These claims, similar to DAC claims, are for claimants who do not qualify for Title 2 benefits on their own earnings record. Since the person does not have their own insured status, the person can file a Title 2 claim on their deceased spouse's record, meaning the deceased spouse is the record holder. The requirements for a DWB claim are complex, so only a knowledgeable representative can determine if you qualify.

28. When Benefits End

If you are approved for benefits, you need to know when your benefits will end so you can plan for that occurrence. Why are benefits ending? When will they end? How will you pay your bills once they end? What happens if you still cannot work?

For Title 2 recipients, your disability insurance benefits will end when you reach full retirement age. At that point, your retirement benefits will begin. You may not notice since the amount should be the same. For Title 16 recipients, if you are "fully insured," SSI will likely also end when retirement benefits begin. If you are not fully insured, they may continue. Your Social Security benefits end once you pass away.

There is one way that benefits can end for any claimant, including child claimants. SSA puts a substantial focus on the potential for medical improvement. For this reason, SSA conducts periodic reviews of people who are receiving benefits. This is called a "Continuing Disability Review" (CDR). If SSA conducts a CDR and determines that your impairments have improved enough to allow you to go back to work, they will stop paying you benefits. For a child claimant, SSI benefits will end if SSA conducts a CDR and determines that the child no longer has two marked limitations or one extreme limitation in the six domains of childhood functioning. For those impairments listed in Chapter 25, medical improvement is not possible, so SSA is unlikely to conduct a CDR in those cases. Unless a person with one of those impairments begins to work at the SGA level, they could collect benefits indefinitely.

When it comes to the termination of benefits, there are some key differences between Title 2 and Title 16. For a Title 2 claim, you can actually try working again *while collecting benefits*! This "Trial

Work Period" (TWP) is actually built into the SSDI regulations because SSA wants to encourage you to try working to see if you can. Therefore, you can work and earn up to a certain amount for up to nine months before your Title 2 benefits will terminate. If, during this time, you cannot sustain work, you can stop and you will not be penalized for trying. Your benefits will just continue. You can then try again later.

But there is a limit to how many times you can start and stop work. If you work and earn a certain amount for any nine months during a rolling 60 month period, you will graduate from the Trial Work Period and your benefits will end since you have demonstrated that you can go back to work. The TWP amount is less than the SGA amount, so it really doesn't take much to reach the TWP threshold. For example, I have already explained that the monthly SGA amount for 2022 is $1,350. For comparison, the TWP earnings amount for 2022 is only $970 per month. This means that in 2022, if you earn less than $970 in a month, that month will not count towards your TWP.

The rolling period for the TWP works the same way as the test to see whether a person is insured. Do you remember when we looked to see if a person had earned a Social Security quarter credit during 20 out of the last 40 quarters? It works the same way for the TWP, but it's nine out of the last 60 months. So, we start today, and we go back 60 months. We ask whether you earned above the TWP amount for *any* nine months during those 60 months. If the answer is yes, the TWP ends. If not, we ask the same question next month. At that point, we have a new month to consider, so the 61st oldest month drops out of consideration.

What this means is you can start working, you can earn $970 or more, and then you can stop working if it's too difficult. You can even do that eight times while continuing to collect SSDI benefits. However, once you reach that amount for the ninth month (and remember the months *do not* need to be consecutive), the TWP will end. Once the TWP ends, you will still get benefits for two more months while you transition out of the Title 2 program, and then those benefits will stop.

The TWP is not there to allow you to earn money while also receiving benefits. Yes, by working you will earn some money, but that is not the purpose of the TWP. It is designed for you to see if you can go back to full time work. However, your participation in a TWP could theoretically be used as evidence during a CDR that you have medically improved. So, if your goal is to get back to work anyway, and you're not concerned about a CDR, the TWP is an excellent opportunity. If you find you can go back to working full time, that's great!

But you should not try to work just so you can earn extra money while also collecting SSDI benefits. If you are working full time, at 160 hours per month, you only need to earn a little over $6 per hour to reach $970. That's less than the federal minimum wage. So, if you are trying to game the system like this, it won't last long. You will reach nine months very quickly, show that you can go back to work, and the benefits you fought for will terminate, probably when you least expect it and when you can least afford it.

For a Title 16 claim, there is no Trial Work Period. If you go back to work, your benefits will immediately terminate. But you should be aware that there are also other ways SSI can terminate. SSI involves benefits funded through regular income taxes, with the idea being that you will use these benefits to pay for basic necessities like food and housing. For this reason, incarceration for more than 12 months will result in termination of those benefits. The logic makes sense. Incarceration means the government is already providing you with basic necessities like food and housing, so you no longer need SSI for these expenses. If you lose SSI benefits due to being incarcerated for more than 12 months, you will have to re-apply for SSI and be found disabled again. If your incarceration lasts less than 12 months, SSI will be suspended during the period of incarceration, and will re-start upon release.

But the more common reason that SSI ends is that a recipient becomes over resourced, with too many assets or too much income to remain eligible for SSI. For SSI, the asset and income tests are never-ending. You need to remain continuously eligible to keep getting SSI. Because the threshold for both assets and income is so low, people often become accidentally over resourced. Someone can become over resourced even if they are paying attention. I have already explained that someone could stay with a friend or family member, and the value of that "free rent" counts against the person's SSI benefits. But keep in mind this is just one example of how someone can accidentally become over resourced.

Here is another example. What happens if an SSI recipient gets married to someone who has assets, or who works and has income over the SSI limits? Maybe this couple did not want to become legally married for fear of losing SSI, but had to so one could access the other's private health insurance. Because the *household* income now includes the income of the spouse, while the claimant's personal asset and income picture has not changed, SSA nevertheless considers the claimant over resourced, and therefore ineligible for SSI. This demonstrates just how unreliable SSI is.

The program is there so you don't become homeless or starve. But it does not always guarantee those things. Still, if you do not have sufficient credits for the SSDI program, and you have no other option, SSI is better than nothing. But just barely. If your benefits terminate for any of these reasons, it will be difficult to get them reinstated. You will most likely need to reapply for benefits from scratch. This means you would need to be found financially eligible for SSI, but also found medically disabled again by SSA.

If you have received SSDI or SSI benefits, and SSA later determines you were not eligible to receive them, for any reason, SSA will issue an "overpayment" letter telling you to repay the benefits. At that point, you have three options. First, you can just agree and repay the overpayment amount, but seldom do people who have been receiving Social Security benefits have thousands of dollars just sitting around. In fact, for SSI recipients, *not* having thousands of dollars was a specific part of your eligibility requirement to begin with!

Second, you could do nothing, but the overpayment does not just go away. SSA will keep the overpayment on your record, and many years later, when you go to file for retirement benefits, SSA will pounce, informing you that they are deducting what you owe from those benefits. Finally, you can challenge the overpayment, saying you do not think you owe the money back, or that you do owe it, but you just cannot afford to repay it. If the reason for the overpayment is your fault (for example, you lied or committed fraud to get the benefits), you will need to repay it. But generally, the claimant is not at fault for causing an overpayment. Still, if you can afford to pay it back, you will be required to do so.

Here is an example. A claimant receiving SSDI benefits goes back to work as part of the TWP. The claimant tells SSA he went back to work, and he reports his earnings, but SSA does not stop the claimant's benefit payments. The claimant is entitled to receive benefits during the nine months of the TWP, and for two additional months as he transitions out of the Title 2 program. That is 11 months total, and then the benefits should stop. However, SSA does not stop the benefits payments, and instead pays the claimant for a total of two years, or 24 months, which is 13 months longer than they should have.

Eventually, SSA will realize what happened, and will let the claimant know he was paid benefits for 13 months when he should not have been. SSA will explain that it wants the extra money back. This is the most common situation. The claimant keeps SSA informed as required, but for some reason there is a delay, and the claimant accidentally gets paid too much. This is not the claimant's fault. Still, if the claimant can afford to repay the overpayment amount, the claimant must do so. To get SSA, or an ALJ, to "waive" the overpayment, and not require that it be paid back, the claimant must not be at fault for causing the overpayment, and must also be unable to pay it back.

To make that determination, SSA will consider the claimant's assets and income, and will also look at "ordinary and necessary living expenses." These include things like rent, car payment, gas, insurance, utilities, clothes, debt repayment, etc. If all of the claimant's income goes to those things, and if the claimant has no substantial savings, SSA can choose to waive the overpayment. If SSA refuses to waive it, the claimant can appeal and ask for a hearing with an ALJ, and then the Judge can choose to waive the overpayment. But a waiver is not guaranteed, so do your best to keep SSA informed about employment, income, and any changes to your financial circumstances. This is particularly important if you are receiving SSI, since it's so easy to suddenly become ineligible.

And if you *know* you should not be receiving the benefits, *leave them alone*! Do not spend them. It isn't free money. If you are not entitled to the money, after you receive the direct deposit, leave it in the bank account and just let it sit there. That way, when SSA does eventually demand that money back, you will be prepared to repay it. You can still challenge the overpayment and say you need that money for ordinary and necessary living expenses, and you just might win that argument.

Here is how that would work. The Judge would review your income and compare it to your ordinary and necessary living expenses. While you are waiting for your hearing, you should keep track of your income and expenses so you are prepared to share that information with the Judge. If you do not have sufficient income each month to cover your basic living expenses, the Judge can waive the overpayment even though you have the overpayment money sitting in a bank account. The reason is that it's not actually your money. In fact, it's money that you were never entitled to receive in the first place.

If you convince the Judge you are running a monthly deficit, the Judge might just waive the overpayment so that you can use that money to pay your monthly bills. This would then put you in the same position as someone who spent the money before asking for the overpayment to be waived. The difference is that in case you lose the argument, you will have the money available and you will be able to immediately repay the overpayment to SSA without difficulty. For those who do not have the money, because they spent it, and are required to repay the overpayment amount, the result is even more financial difficulty than the person was in prior to applying for benefits. Now, instead of asking SSA for money, *you owe them money*! It's best to prevent that situation if you can.

One final note about "overpayment" cases. These are considered *non-disability* cases because the issue is not whether you were medically disabled. In these cases, the issues are whether you were eligible to receive the benefits, whether you were at fault for causing an overpayment, and whether you can afford to repay the overpayment. There is no medical determination for these cases. There are no past due benefits or ongoing monthly benefits at issue either. For these cases, benefits have already been paid to the claimant. Because there are no past due benefits, there is no way for a representative to collect a fee using a fee agreement. It is therefore difficult to find a representative. As a result, for these cases, claimants typically appear at the hearing without representation.

You could ask your former representative to help you, but this is a new case and they would have long ago collected the original fee. It is unlikely that the former representative would want to spend time helping you out for free. Some might, but it's rare. For these cases, try to get a representative if you can, but do not be surprised if you can't find someone who will accept your case. You may need to come to the hearing without representation. If this happens, be prepared to discuss why the overpayment happened, and be prepared to share your income and your ordinary and necessary living expenses with the Judge. It may seem like the Judge is prying into your private life when discussing what you spend on food, rent, utilities, and clothes each month, but the law requires the Judge to analyze that information and compare it to your income. If you want the overpayment waived, you have to go through that process.

29. Firing Your Representative

If you are unhappy with the way your representative is representing you, you do not have to keep that person around. You can fire a representative at any time. However, just as there is a specific process for hiring a representative, so too there is a specific process for firing one.

As I explained in Chapter 5, most claimants who hire a representative will sign a fee agreement that allows the claimant to automatically pay the representative from the past due benefits, and the representative to get their fee without having to hassle or chase the claimant. However, you can only ever have one active fee agreement. This means that to fire your representative *and* be able to sign a new fee agreement with a new representative, you must follow a specific procedure.

Because you cannot have two fee agreements with two different representatives at the same time, when firing a representative, you need to have the first fee agreement canceled. If you fire a representative, you need to ask them to file a document in your case withdrawing from the case *and* also waiving their right to collect a fee. That second part is very important because it invalidates the fee agreement you signed with the fired representative. Without this second part, the fee agreement stays in place, meaning that if you sign a fee agreement with a different representative, that second fee agreement cannot be approved by the Judge. This means that the second representative will have a hard time being paid for their services, which of course means that you may have difficulty finding someone different to represent you.

So why would the first representative, who you are firing, agree to give up a fee, even after having already done some work on the case? Because that person may not want to continue doing more work if they think their client is not going to cooperate, and the lack of cooperation will result in a denial of benefits. Remember, the representative only gets paid if you get a favorable decision. If the representative thinks that you, the client, may cause an unfavorable outcome because of a bad attitude, a desire to not cooperate with the Judge, not assisting with obtaining your medical records, etc., then it does not matter how much time they have spent on the case. They will just want out before they waste any more time. They have other clients, and they would rather spend time on those potentially winnable cases.

For this reason, you can approach the representative and explain you do not think the relationship is a good fit, and most representatives will agree to withdraw. The representative can also choose to withdraw from your case at any time if they do not want to continue representing you. Either way, the representative can either decide to waive the right to collect a fee, or can try to collect a fee. In order to collect a fee, the representative would need to file a fee petition, where they explain the work they did on your case and ask SSA to approve a fee even though they no longer represent you.

If you cannot get the representative to waive the right to collect a fee, and you still want them gone, you can still fire them. But in that circumstance, you will need to tell the new representative what happened with the first representative. The new representative can still represent you, but to be paid by SSA, they will also need to file a fee petition. You should make sure the new representative is okay with doing that. Filing a fee petition is more work because the representative must justify the fee rather than collecting it automatically based on a fee agreement.

But if there is a former representative who has refused to waive the right to collect a fee, the new representative will have no choice. Most representatives will understand that process, and if they think you have a winnable case, they may agree to take it even though they will have to file a fee petition afterward. But some representatives do not want to engage in the complex fee petition process, so you may have some difficulty finding a new representative. A fee petition will not impact whether you get a favorable decision or not, it's simply an alternative way for the representative(s) to be paid. It is most often used when there is no valid fee agreement. Remember, you cannot have two fee agreements with different representatives, so if you do that, both are invalid and will be denied by the Judge.

This is really an issue between the representatives and SSA, it's not something you have to worry much about. However, if the potential new representative asks you whether you signed a fee agreement with someone else, you need to be honest with them. This is their job, and they want to be paid fairly for their time. It's only fair to let that person know that there is a fee agreement lingering out there. That way they know they cannot get paid via a fee agreement, and they will need to do a fee petition instead. Then, that representative can make an informed decision whether to accept your case.

If you approach a representative and ask that person to withdraw but that person tries to convince you otherwise, or outright refuses to withdraw from your case, you don't need to worry. It's your case and you have the right to have the representative you want. You can write a simple letter to the Judge, and mail it, fax it, or bring it to the hearing office. This is a very informal process. All the letter needs to say is that you no longer want to be represented by that person. The representative may refuse to waive the right to collect a fee, but they cannot force you to keep them as your representative. You get to decide who represents you.

Regardless of who your representative is, remember this is *your* case, not theirs. *You* are the person who has gone through the pain and agony of your impairments and been unable to work. *You* are the person who has worked and earned those Social Security credits. *You* are the person who is entitled to, and deserving of, disability benefits. *You* are the person who is taking the time to see medical sources, gather documentation, and file the claim. The representative works for you. This is your case, and you are in charge.

PART 6: Improving the Outcome for You and for Everyone Else

30. The Outcome is Largely Beyond Your Control

The title of this chapter may be very difficult for you to read, but at this point it also probably comes as no surprise. There is nothing you can do about the office politics, the way cases are assigned, conflicting incentives, congressional priorities, etc. You cannot influence the state agency officials, the way the consultative examiners write their reports, or which hearing office your case is assigned to. You cannot choose which Judge you get, how biased the Judge is, or when during the month the decision is drafted, edited, or signed. You have no say which Attorney Advisor decision writer drafts your decision, how close that person is to being fired for poor production, or how close the hearing office is to reaching its monthly goal. You cannot control who the HOCALJ is, who the management team is, or how they operate.

Since you cannot control any of this, it is also stuff that you don't need to worry about! You should be aware of it, which is why you have taken the time to read this book, but you do not need to stress out about things you cannot control. This is, of course, much easier said than done. There will inevitably be things that transpire along the way that cause you a lot of stress. Denials at the initial and reconsideration levels are understandably stressful, but so is finding out you will then have to wait more than a year to have your hearing with an Administrative Law Judge. An unfavorable decision from that Judge is stressful, but somehow, it's way more stressful if, when reading that decision, you feel the Judge essentially called you a liar or a fake.

When you truly believe you are disabled and unable to do full time work, and when you have been trying to convince Social Security of this for more than two years, it must be extremely frustrating to have someone who does not know you tell you that you *can* work. I cannot begin to imagine how much more frustrating that situation would be if the rationale ignores thousands of pages of medical records and denies your claim because one time you mentioned that you like to garden, or go on a hike, or go camping. Or you are denied because a doctor who saw you for a grand total of 10 minutes (the consultative examiner) determined you could do work that you know you cannot do.

But as I said, there is simply nothing you can do about any of that. All you can do is seek medical care, present the best case you possibly can, use all the tools at your disposal, and try not to take personally any of the commentary in the decision. Remember, most of that decision is being written by someone who may not even agree with the ultimate outcome. In other words, most likely, the Judge did not misconstrue your words. It was far more likely an Attorney Advisor decision writer who did that. And, most likely, it was done to satisfy a Judge who does not have the medical impairments that you have, and who gets paid way more than you, to sit in a chair all day and take credit for other people's work. No one has a personal slight against you. And remember, the more seemingly inaccurate the decision is, the better it is for you, because a bad decision is more likely to be reversed by the Appeals Council or by a Federal Court.

There are some other ways that people try to be active participants in the case, feeling this will reduce their stress. But these often don't work, because again, you are dealing with a system over which you have little control. For example, some people think that if they contact their members of Congress, this will help them be approved for benefits. This is untrue.

This is called a "Congressional Inquiry," but it's not a useful tool. Members of Congress have absolutely no authority to push

SSA towards any specific outcome. Actually, this is a good thing for claimants, because if members of Congress did have any sway, it would likely not be in your favor. In the big picture of the federal budget, most members of Congress like finding ways to save the taxpayer money. This translates to making sure SSA pays fewer cases, and reviews those that are paid to make sure things were done correctly. This is why the Appeals Council randomly selects favorable cases for review, and why I was assigned to do reviews of hearing offices or Judges that were paying too many cases.

But you don't need to worry, this will not have any direct impact on your specific case. While Congress generally likes to see lower approval numbers overall, SSA decides hundreds of thousands of cases each year, and around half are approved at some point along the way. Congress simply cannot monitor each case, nor do they care to do so. This means the Judges are, at the very least, independent of that type of political interference.

What Representatives and Senators can do is send an inquiry to SSA on behalf of a constituent. If you contact the office of your U.S. Representative or U.S. Senator, you will likely never speak to the actual person who is elected from your district or state. Most likely, you will speak with a staff member in charge of "constituent services." All that person can do is send a letter to the federal agency asking for a status update, and requesting the case be heard as soon as possible. SSA will label those cases as having a Congressional Inquiry, so that after the decision is issued, whatever it may be, the Congressional office involved is informed the case was completed. But the case is not prioritized, you will not have a hearing faster, and you do not have better odds of being approved.

So, you can complain to your Representative or Senator if you want, and it's their job (or, more accurately, the job of the

208

person who handles constituent services) to care enough to do something for you. However, you will not achieve your desired result. Your odds of a favorable outcome and the timeline to get there will not change one bit. And no, this fact does not change in an election year. For the U.S. House of Representatives, every two years is an election year. Those officials are constantly facing re-election, meaning they are always needing to fundraise and campaign. Your disability case is simply not their priority.

31. Get Ready for a Fight

I won't sugarcoat this. If you are going to apply for Social Security Disability benefits, you need to be ready for a fight. The Social Security Disability process is not for the faint of heart. It's long, there are lots of twists and turns, and there are substantial highs and lows. In the previous chapter, I told you all the ways you have no control over the outcome of your case. But I also explained that around half of all cases are approved at some point along the way. So, you can flip a coin and hope for the best, or you can be an active participant and fight for the benefits you believe that you deserve.

This can be a very difficult process for someone who has a high level of education, medical insurance to establish a good treatment record, and the mental wherewithal to endure a slow, drawn-out process. Now remove the financial means, the formal education, and the good medical insurance, and throw in some physical and mental health symptoms that cause difficulty functioning even in the most basic circumstances. As you can imagine, this process can be difficult for many claimants, and is absolutely unbearable for some.

On top of all that, the SSA regulations are completely stacked against you. You need to be prepared for a fight of two years or more, with little or no income, and likely no health insurance (since, in the United States, most people get health insurance from their employer). This means that during this time, you not only have no income, but limited means for medical treatment. This, of course, makes the treatment more expensive, and at a time when you can least afford the higher level of expense. That's right, SSA regulations require you to not work, but to get a lot of medical treatment, even though not working means your access to treatment is severely restricted, or possibly entirely cut off. Because of this, claimants need to learn how to live simple lives, spending little money on anything other than shelter, food, and medical care. A low cost living situation is key, especially because you might not win in the end.

This is why many claimants live in an apartment, rather than in a single family home. Typically, apartment complexes without elevators are cheaper, because elevators are expensive to maintain, and because Americans generally prefer elevators to stairs. Therefore, many claimants end up living on the third floor of a building without an elevator. But those claimants are in for a surprise at the hearing. Judges like to ask about your living situation. Don't be surprised when the decision says you are exaggerating your knee or back impairment because you "chose" to live in a third floor apartment with a lot of stairs.

This is what I mean when I say the whole process is stacked against the claimant. You do what you have to do to survive, and the Judge can, and often will, hold that against you. No medical insurance? You didn't get enough treatment, so you must not be in pain. Third floor apartment? I guess you can walk up and down stairs without a problem. This is why I call it a fight. It's a fight against the government, and common sense is not a factor.

Perhaps you have considered this possibility, or you truly cannot make it up the apartment stairs, so instead you choose to stay in your modest, 800 square foot, single family home, which has no stairs. But this costs more, so to pay the rent you find a job where you earn slightly more than $1,350 per month, the SGA amount for 2022. In that case, the Judge will deny your claim at Step 1 of the sequential evaluation process because you earned too much money.

If that happens, the Judge may not even ask you *any* questions about your medical impairments.

Alright, now let's say you considered that as well, so you choose instead to stay on a family member's couch while you await a decision on your SSI claim. Oops! You just received "free rent," which may reduce your SSI benefits. It's like you just can't win. It almost seems that Congress and SSA have designed the program this way.

This is, again, why I strongly recommend having a representative to guide you and to represent your interests throughout the process. It does not matter whether this person is an attorney or a non-attorney representative who has been vetted by SSA and deemed qualified to represent you. What matters is that you have someone on your side who knows all of SSA's rules and processes, and who will be honest and forthcoming. You need professional guidance so you do not accidentally do something that will hurt your chances of being approved for benefits, or even worse, disqualify you completely.

You need an honest assessment of the things you have done in the past, as well as someone who can guide you, so you know what to do *and not do* in the future. You also may need someone who looks you in the eye and says, "You won't be approved. The disability regulations are not on your side." These words will undoubtedly be hard to hear. But it's better to hear these words before the battle, and to be able to move on with your life in whatever way you can without enduring a two-year fight that the representative knows would be a losing endeavor.

The important thing here is knowing. You need someone on your team who will be honest with you. Many people will just stop working and then file a claim, assuming that because they think they

212

cannot continue at their previous job, their claim will be swiftly approved. Because they refer to themselves as "disabled," and perhaps friends and family members may use the same term, the entire support group for the claimant is shocked when the claim is denied, when the Judge decides the claimant *can* work.

Therefore, clearly, it's not a good idea to just stop working, file an application, and assume you will be approved. Since you bought and are reading this book, that likely isn't your situation! Or it was and you are now learning why that was not a good move. The Social Security Disability process requires very specific evidence. You cannot just slip through the cracks and be accidentally approved. Things just don't work that way. You need a representative who can provide an honest assessment of your case, and who will work within SSA's rules and regulations to set you up for the best possible outcome. No one can guarantee you will be approved, but you will be much better off in this process with a qualified, professional representative who is ready for the fight and who knows the battlefield and the opponent much better than you do.

Here is another example of why it's so important to have a representative. I have explained to you how you can become accidentally over resourced and disqualified from receiving SSI. But there is some good news. There are many local, state, and federal government programs that provide nutrition and housing support to people with minimal income, and SSA does not count that support as income. Therefore, you can apply for and receive those benefits and it will not count against your SSI benefits. These programs are listed in the Social Security Administration's Program Operations Manual System (POMS). However, like the regulations, the POMS is incredibly detailed and SSA's rules are complex, so you need a knowledgeable representative who can research and interpret the

POMS provisions to see if any benefits you are currently receiving, or plan to apply for, would make you ineligible for SSI benefits.

Even if you have a representative, and you do everything you can to present the best possible case, if you then get an unfavorable decision, was it all just a complete waste of time? Definitely not! A qualified representative will also have experience reviewing the Judge's decision and preparing an appeal to the Appeals Council. A representative will help you understand that you should not take the contents of the decision personally. As I have said, the Judge and the Attorney Advisor decision writer have no grudge against you. They have their own production metrics to be worried about. They are concerned with getting your case prepared and heard, and your decision drafted and signed. They just want the case closed, and they do not care what happens to you after that.

Shockingly, this can also be good news. When someone does not really care about the contents of the document being drafted, it can often be sloppy and contain errors. A representative knows what to look for when reading a decision. That person knows when evidence was evaluated incorrectly. Each medical opinion in the medical record must be addressed in the decision, with sufficient supporting rationale. Your representative will be able to dive deep into the specific arguments presented in the decision and will know if something was done improperly.

Of course, having a representative does not take away your responsibility to also review the decision. After all, this is *your* decision, and it directly impacts *your* life. Representatives represent a lot of clients, and they read a lot of decisions. While they are professionals, and their opinion matters a lot, remember that they are reviewing your decision *in addition to* you, not *instead of* you. There is no substitute for reviewing your own decision. Think critically about every sentence in the decision. Remember that the Judge did not write most of those sentences. Most of the decision is computer-generated language, or was written by an attorney whose job it is to write the decision the Judge wants, even if such a decision is difficult to justify. I wrote hundreds of decisions that were difficult to write for this reason.

In fact, there may be a benefit to having someone who disagrees with the Judge's decision write that decision. No one at SSA will admit that this happens, but it does. Some Attorney Advisor decision writers who feel a decision is wrong, unsupported, and therefore impossible to draft due to lack of supporting evidence, will sometimes plant intentional errors into the decision to make it more easily appealable for the claimant. Sometimes this is on purpose, to scuttle the decision, and sometimes it is just unavoidable when there simply isn't sufficient evidence to justify the outcome the Judge wants.

Here is an example. We have a claimant with a back disorder. The medical record contains opinions from state agency medical consultants (those are the doctors that review the medical record but never see the claimant) suggesting the claimant can do light work on a full time basis. We also have opinions from a consultative examiner (that is the doctor that sees the claimant one time for around 10 minutes) and several of the claimant's treating doctors. All of these other medical opinions state the claimant is unable to sustain a full time work schedule. Likely, some of those treating source opinions came into the record at the hearing level, after the state agency medical consultants wrote their opinions.

However, the Judge just doesn't like the claimant's case for whatever reason, and he instructs the Attorney Advisor decision writer to draft a decision that will find the claimant not disabled. The

Judge, of course, chooses to accept the opinions of the state agency medical consultants over all other opinions throughout the record that suggest the claimant cannot do full time work. But, as is often the case, the Judge does not explain why, forcing the Attorney Advisor decision writer to come up with rationale and justification for an unjustifiable decision.

If the Attorney Advisor decision writer wants to give the claimant something to work with on appeal so the decision has a better chance of being overturned, the attorney *could* use a lot of conclusory statements. This means the decision will talk about how the older state agency medical consultant opinions are more persuasive than the newer opinions, but not explain *why* they are more persuasive.

But if you think about it, this doesn't make any sense. Why would older, outdated opinions be more persuasive than newer opinions based on more medical evidence? Also, why would the opinions of doctors who never examined the claimant be more persuasive than the opinions of treating doctors who see the claimant often? The Attorney Advisor decision writer will say that those older opinions from doctors who never saw the claimant are "consistent with other medical evidence in the record" without explaining what that "other" evidence is. This is just a conclusion without a citation, so no one knows what "other medical evidence" this refers to. Often, there is no such "other" evidence anywhere in the medical record.

Why do this? The Attorney Advisor decision writer *may* want to thwart the decision and give the claimant an appealable issue, or may just have no better way to say something that is unsupported by the evidence. A statement that a medical opinion is consistent with "other" medical evidence is only good rationale if the writer explains what that "other" evidence is. But if the attorney cannot describe the other evidence, this argument is meaningless.

This provides an issue the claimant can use for the appeal. The claimant can argue the decision is not supported by substantial evidence, saying the Judge did not provide a good enough justification for accepting the older state agency medical consultant opinions over the opinions from so many other doctors that have actually examined and treated the claimant. The Appeals Council will likely agree and send the case back to the Judge to consider those newer opinions that are all consistent with each other. Of course, the only real way to fully "consider" that evidence is to give it the persuasive credit it deserves and approve the claim. While there is no guarantee of this on appeal, at least that claimant gets a second chance to present their case, possibly to a different Judge.

As I said, sometimes an Attorney Advisor decision writer will include an appealable issue on purpose, and other times it's just an unavoidable consequence of a ridiculous and unsupported decision. After being drafted, the decision does, of course, then go to the Judge to be edited, at which point the Judge can add their own rationale. The Judge could also remove the appealable content placed into the decision by the Attorney Advisor decision writer. This means there is no guarantee that intentionally added language will remain in the final decision. But the Judges move very quickly, so artfully disguised language that appears to be making the Judge's point, but which does so in a conclusory manner that lacks a solid flow of logic, will often slip through the cracks and make it into the decision that is mailed to the claimant.

So, you may receive an unfavorable decision that contains gaps in logic, conclusory statements, or outright misses or misinterprets evidence. It's not a favorable decision, but it's better than nothing. At least you're being handed appealable issues. This may have been the intention of the Attorney Advisor decision writer who is trying to help you, it may be an oversight, or the attorney who wrote the decision may have had no choice because there was just no good evidence to support an unfavorable decision. You'll never know, and it doesn't matter anyway. Whatever the reason, you now have something to use to try and get the case sent back for a new hearing. And if this is the second unfavorable decision from the same Judge, you will be guaranteed a new Judge the next time around.

Of course, I know you want to avoid this situation. No one wants to have to appeal. You want to win your case the first time. To increase your chances of that, you need to know what is in your medical records and make sure your doctors understand your intent to apply for Social Security Disability benefits. A doctor who does not agree with your desire to do so can undermine your application by filling out a functional capacity form indicating you can work. If the record contains a medical opinion like that from a treating source who knows you well, the result will almost certainly be an unfavorable decision.

So be sure to mention anything and everything relevant to your disability claim to your doctor at every visit and make sure it is all well documented. Many providers, especially alternative sources such as chiropractors, massage therapists, acupuncturists, counselors, etc., may not routinely keep extensive written records, but you need them to do so for your case! Remember, you can ask to see your records at any time to be sure the documentation is being done well. You cannot tell a doctor, or any other source, *what* to write in their reports, but you can make sure they are *doing* those reports. You can make sure they are documenting your symptoms, any treatment, any

218

observations, objective tests they perform, and your functional abilities and limitations. This is all necessary when it comes time to file and support your disability claim.

Diagnoses are necessary for the Judge to find that you have a medically determinable impairment. Remember, this is a very low bar at Step 2 of the sequential evaluation process. But you also need to show functional limitations to support your disability claim. This is what the Judge will use to develop your RFC. It is important to show evidence documenting your symptoms and the specific way that they impact your ability to work. Also keep in mind that while medical opinions are important, these alone are insufficient to prove that you are disabled. Those opinions must be supported by observations, test results, and objective evidence, like x-rays and MRI studies. This support is necessary for the Judge to find that a medical opinion is persuasive.

A doctor saying "my patient cannot work 40 hours per week" without any support, justification, or rationale, is essentially worthless for your disability claim. Such an opinion will be considered unpersuasive because the Judge does not know *why* the doctor said that, which means the Judge cannot trust the validity of the opinion. While opinions are important, so are the observations, test results, and other objective evidence that backs them up. In other words, the Judge needs to know *what* a doctor thinks, but also *why* the doctor thinks that. The *why* is extremely important.

For this reason, a comprehensive medical record is crucial. It's your job to have your record be as complete as possible. Yes, a representative can help you get medical records, and yes, SSA should also try to help out with that. But there is no substitute for you taking charge and keeping watch over your own case. Know your medical sources, know how many medical opinions there are, and know what else is in your medical files. Each time you see a doctor, review the "after visit summary" and make sure that source has your conditions, medications, and allegations correctly listed. The bottom line is *you* need to make sure that *your* records are accurate. If you don't, no one else will.

32. Don't DIY Your Disability Claim

If, after reading this book, you feel like you can now tackle this process on your own, I strongly encourage you to reconsider finding a qualified representative. I have not even scratched the surface when it comes to the mindboggling complexity of the SSA regulations. I would like to present a specific, yet complicated example of why this is so important. This is a very detailed situation, so please bear with me, but these circumstances are typical of what Social Security Judges see on a regular basis, and all this detail is necessary to illustrate my point. At the end of this example, you will see why this person wins her case if she has a representative, and loses her case if she doesn't.

Let's consider a claimant who is 49 years of age. This person, as is common with applicants, has both physical and mental impairments, and feels she can no longer work. The most common impairments are musculoskeletal and mental in nature, so for this example, the claimant has degenerative discs in the lower lumbar spine that make it very painful to stand or walk for more than a few minutes at a time. This claimant also has anxiety and depression. She is denied twice by the state agency at the initial and reconsideration levels, and she requests a hearing with an Administrative Law Judge.

The claimant turns 50 while waiting for the hearing, something that happens more often than you would think. She has a lot of anxiety when it comes to being around other people, which is the reason she keeps quitting jobs as a restaurant server, the only type of job she has worked during the past 20 years. She has back pain, but it came on so gradually throughout her 40s that she usually does not think much about it. Even so, she cannot afford to see an orthopedic specialist because she has no health insurance. SSA did,

221

however, send her to see a doctor (the consultative examiner) who did an x-ray and a quick exam, which were paid for by SSA. The claimant did not want to go to that appointment because she would miss work, but she was told she had to go or her claim for Social Security Disability benefits would be denied, so she attended reluctantly.

When this unrepresented claimant gets to the hearing, and the Judge asks why she cannot work, she immediately starts talking about how anxious she gets when she leaves home to go to work. She explains she is working part time in a restaurant, earning just $500 per month. The claimant also explains she has a hard time managing demanding customers, which further causes her anxiety to flare. As I said, when it comes to why she cannot work, the claimant considers her anxiety to be more significant than her back pain. This is common. Many claimants over the age of 50, who do not have a representative, get to the hearing and immediately start discussing anxiety or depression, trying to convince the Judge this is why that person cannot work. This is what this claimant truly believes to be the case, so she is being honest as she presents her case to the Judge. But a qualified, experienced representative would have known *not to do this!*

Had this claimant hired a representative, that person would have known that the regulations direct that a person who is 50 years of age, who has past relevant work at the light exertional level (restaurant server is light work due to substantial standing and walking), and who is limited to sedentary work, should be found disabled according to the grid rules. The claimant did not think her back pain was significant, but the representative knows better. The claimant went to the consultative examination appointment because she was told she had to, but she did not think about it after that. It

222

turns out that the consultative examiner who saw her reviewed the x-ray, noted that the claimant has moderate to severe degenerative disc disease, and stated that in his medical opinion, the claimant is limited to sedentary work. However, the claimant never read that report.

The representative knows that this medical opinion is unchallenged in the record, and a favorable decision can be achieved if the claimant amends, or changes, her alleged onset date (AOD), the day she is saying her disability began. Sometimes, a represented claimant will amend the AOD forward in time to coincide with the evidence, thus transforming a possible partially favorable, later onset decision into a fully favorable decision. This happens because instead of the EOD being later than the AOD, the AOD is moved forward in time to be the same date as the EOD. A representative may suggest this specifically so the decision can be fully favorable. Judges like fully favorable decisions because the hearings can be shorter and because those decisions require less time to draft. However, it's important to note that only represented claimants can amend the AOD. This is something that an unrepresented claimant is not allowed to do because this can only be done on the advice of counsel.

In this case, all the represented claimant has to do is amend the AOD to her 50th birthday. Then, the representative can make an argument to the Judge that the claimant is disabled beginning on that date without any discussion of the claimant's anxiety impairment. This is because the claimant would be 50 years of age, should be found limited to sedentary work based on the consultative examiner's opinion, and has no past relevant work at the sedentary level. Thus, the grid rules apply and the claimant should be found disabled. The anxiety impairment is irrelevant.

This is an easy case for the representative to argue. In fact, this is a common scenario, and most representatives have no difficulty convincing Judges to approve cases with similar circumstances. Represented claimants amend the AOD to a 50th or 55th birthday often, and those cases tend to be approved with little hassle, even by Judges with low approval rates. In fact, the claimant likely would not have even needed to testify. The Judge would have conducted a short hearing to have the vocational expert classify the past relevant work as light work, and the hearing would be over. The grid rules direct a finding of disabled, so it's an easy decision for the Judge once the AOD is amended to the 50th birthday.

The claimant would be found disabled and would get monthly benefits, a little bit of past due benefits (some of which goes to pay the representative's fee), and likely the case would not be reviewed during a CDR due to the claimant's age (CDRs are less common for claimants over 50). This means the claimant would be able to collect Social Security benefits starting at age 50, instead of having to wait for retirement benefits to begin. Thankfully that person hired a representative!

If she had not, here is what would have unfortunately happened. The Judge is supposed to be independent and apply the regulations fairly. Thus, most Judges would see the x-ray, note the claimant's age, and consider the possibility of a partially favorable decision. Specifically, in that situation, the Judge would consider a later onset decision, finding the claimant not disabled while she was 49 years of age, but becoming disabled at her 50th birthday. So far, it sounds like the claimant did not need a representative to reach this outcome, right?

Here is the difference between the two scenarios. Unless a decision is fully favorable, the Judge is required to hold a full hearing, which often lasts an hour or more. At that hearing, the claimant will need to testify. The only way the decision for this particular case can be fully favorable is if the claimant amends the alleged onset date, which she cannot do since she is now unrepresented. This means the decision cannot be fully favorable, a hearing is necessary, and the claimant will need to testify.

Who knows what the claimant would say during that testimony! Remember, she did not think her back pain was significant. So, when the Judge asks if she can stand and walk enough to do the server job, perhaps she says something like, "Yeah, I sometimes work as a server, when I can." And there it is. The claimant just acknowledged that she can, in fact, do the server job, which is classified as light work by the DOT. That testimony provides the Judge with the evidence he needs to find that the claimant can do her past relevant work.

The claimant chose to not have a representative who could have helped her amend the AOD and cruise to a fully favorable decision. Instead, she chose to have a hearing and to testify. Because she did not know the law, because she did not know what to say and what not to say, she said something that caused the Judge to deny her claim. This claimant wanted to do this herself so she could save $6,000 in a representative fee, and instead she lost tens of thousands of dollars in future benefits! This was a very expensive mistake. The only difference between these two scenarios is the presence of a qualified, knowledgeable, and professional Social Security Disability representative. Yes, the representative earned a fee for his services, a total of 25% of the past due benefits. Still, the claimant would have received the other 75% of her past due benefits, and benefits every month starting at age 50. Seems worth it to me!

Please, do not try and do this on your own. I have explained the five-step sequential evaluation process, who writes the decision, how the case moves through the system, and all of the incentives (good and bad) that employees encounter on a daily basis. You now have more knowledge than most claimants. But this is a legal process, and you need a representative on your side for you to achieve the best possible result in your case.

I recommend finding a representative who can sit down with you and talk face-to-face. A local representative who knows the Judges in your local hearing office, where your case is likely to be sent, is the best choice. I am not a member of the National Organization of Social Security Disability Representatives (NOSSCR, https://nosscr.org) and I receive nothing by mentioning them. But I do know this is an organization that helps people find a representative specifically for a Social Security Disability claim. At the top of their home page, you will see "LAWYER REFERRAL SERVICE." If you have no other leads, this would be a good place to start. You can also do an internet search for "Social Security Disability representative" along with your city or town, or a medium to large size city close to where you live.

33. Fraud, Waste, and Abuse

Something that tends to bother and stress claimants is the feeling that throughout this process, they are "part of the problem." There are uninformed people who will tell claimants that anyone who files for *welfare* is not only draining taxpayer resources, but also committing *fraud* by alleging inability to work full time. They will say that we all have some pain we work through, yet we don't all ask the government for money. Further, these same people may tell you that if you are denied and you appeal, you are *wasting* taxpayer money by dragging out the process. In many parts of the country, you may even hear someone describe what you are doing as an *abuse* of the system. It can be very stressful to hear these opinions. And they are just that, opinions.

Hearing your actions described this way may cause you to second-guess your decision to apply for Social Security Disability benefits. Do I really need government help? Maybe I can just work through the pain? Am I stealing taxpayer money? If you are asking yourself these questions, I encourage you to remember that you are *entitled* to these benefits so long as you qualify. That is why some people refer to them as *entitlements*. You have paid into the system for many years, and you have the right to receive these benefits. This applies to both Title 2 benefits, which are funded through the OASDI tax, and to Title 16 benefits, which are funded through regular income taxes. If you work, you have paid for both programs for a long time, and those programs are there for you if and when you need them.

So, when you do end up needing these benefits, you should apply for them without feeling doubt or remorse. You did not choose to be sick or injured, it just happened. You worked when you could work, and now that you cannot, the Social Security Disability program is there for you. That what it's for. Comments like those above are beyond your control. Ignorant people will say what they will say. Try not to let these comments bother you, as they have no impact on your case. But I do want to help you understand what these terms mean, why they are so loaded, and why they really have no place in a discussion about Social Security Disability.

You may sometimes see a news article published about someone who was caught lying and defrauding Social Security. The article is likely highly sensationalized. The story might sound something like this: A person is seen eating lobster every night, after being caught entering a Social Security office using a neck brace and a walker, only to go back out into the parking lot and lift the walker into the back of a minivan like it weighs nothing. It's easy to see why a media outlet would run that story. It's unbelievable that someone would do that! But the reason this is news is specifically because this situation is so out of the ordinary.

It is true that a very, *very* small number of claimants have intentionally defrauded SSA over the years. There was also a major event in West Virginia that was uncovered around 10 years ago involving a corrupt Judge, a devious attorney representative, and a dishonest doctor. The three of them were working together to create a favorable decision factory. Here is how it worked. The doctor would see the claimant and produce phony medical records. The Judge would assign himself this representative's cases. The Judge would then cite the phony medical reports as justification for the favorable decisions. The attorney would get paid the normal fee of 25% of past due benefits, and would then give kickbacks to the doctor and the Judge.

Because of the sheer volume of cases they handled together over many years, this trio ended up stealing a lot of money. Yet, most of the claimants involved never even knew the corruption was happening. They believed they were disabled, the medical evaluation was legitimate, and the Judge was just being fair by finding them disabled. Eventually, the crime ring was discovered, and all parties involved were prosecuted. The representative who was the mastermind of the operation was sentenced to a very long term in federal prison. The Judge died in prison as well.

These situations do exist. There are bad Judges, bad doctors, and bad lawyers who are dishonest and who steal from United States taxpayers. But the West Virginia situation made the news because it was literally the largest scam in the history of Social Security. In other words, this was such a big news story when the scheme was uncovered specifically because this situation is so far outside anything that happens on a day-to-day basis. Apple TV even made a documentary about it!

There are a few dishonest people who think they can get away with doing this, but thankfully, not many. At $6,000 per case for the lawyer, or a couple thousand dollars per month in benefits for the claimant, there's just not enough money for most people to take such a risk. The amount of money and time a person needs to spend building their medical record for a disability claim is substantial. That person could just work, expend less effort, and earn more money without risking going to federal prison. The West Virginia scheme involved thousands of cases over a period of many years. But for a single claimant to try and defraud SSA, for most people it just isn't worth the risk. So, while you may have heard the term "fraud, waste, and abuse," in reality, none of these things is a significant problem.

To further illustrate why this is the case, we need to separate these three words and examine each one separately. What I have been discussing thus far falls under the first word, *fraud*. This is a fairly objective term, meaning someone is knowingly and intentionally fabricating evidence, lying in their application, lying under oath at the hearing, etc. While this does happen, it's extremely rare, although some people are caught in the act.

SSA actually has an investigative team responsible for cracking these cases. At some point, someone within SSA who suspects fraud will refer the situation to that team, and a law enforcement agent will conduct surveillance of the claimant at home, at work, or just moving around town. The person will then make contact with and interview the claimant to see if the allegations presented in the disability application are legitimate.

For example, let's say the claimant alleges disability because that person cannot stand or walk well. The record also contains observations by a doctor of a claimant walking with a limp. Still, someone at SSA thinks this may be false, either because another doctor did not observe the limp, or perhaps the person visited a Social Security office and was observed to be walking normally by SSA staff. Sometimes a doctor will see someone walk with a limp in the examination room, but notice that once the person leaves the office, they seem to walk differently. When the person goes outside and walks to their car, and they do not think anyone is still watching, the person will suddenly walk normally. If such a situation is documented, that would be good reason to refer the case to the investigative team.

The investigator will observe the claimant without that person's knowledge, following the claimant for a few hours on a random day, to see if that person is limping. If the claimant can walk

230

just fine, the investigator will then make contact, and see if that person is feigning a limp at that time, once the claimant now knows that someone is watching. Perhaps that person is faking a limp, but there could also be a reasonable explanation. Maybe the claimant has an improving condition, or perhaps the person uses pain medication that makes it easier to walk right after using the medication, but less well as it wears off. So, while that person may be trying to seem worse by acting, there could also be a reasonable explanation for the observed behaviors.

Still, in my experience, these reports almost always suggest the person is lying. The investigators who do these checks want to find things, that's their whole job. They rarely give the person being investigated the benefit of the doubt. They also, despite having no substantial medical or mental health training, behave like they can establish medical facts. For example, if a person has alleged mental health impairments, the report might say something about how the person "was able to have a normal conversation," thereby suggesting the person does not have a severe mental health condition, and that the person is clearly committing fraud.

But what is a *normal* conversation? This is something that a psychologist or a psychiatrist is trained to recognize, but not a law enforcement officer. Police are not trained on how to recognize or deal with mental health impairments. Thus, much of these reports is pure speculation. The only sources who can determine whether a person is "faking" a condition are medical sources who have the education, training, and experience to recognize what is genuine behavior and what is not.

Because these reports almost always suggest the claimant is lying, Judges who want to deny such cases cite to these reports as evidence of deception even when there is good evidence from a mental health specialist supporting the claimant's allegations. We then have competing evidence from a psychologist and a police officer. Which source is better trained and equipped to determine whether the claimant's mental health allegations are genuine? A mental health specialist, who is trained to detect lying, determined the claimant's allegations are genuine. But just to make sure, let's call in a police officer trained in how to suspect, subdue, and arrest someone. It makes no sense.

I cannot remember ever reading one of these investigative reports that suggested the claimant was telling the truth, and not defrauding SSA. In the same way that the Appeals Council has to continuously justify its own existence, these investigators have to continuously find fraud. Otherwise, why have them? So, in the end, these reports are basically just self-fulfilling prophecies. If you want to show the person is committing fraud, just refer them for an investigation and you will get the evidence you need to show fraud. They almost always end with the conclusion that the person is faking a condition, committing fraud, and trying to steal government benefits.

But what is not fraud is someone who legitimately feels disabled, and is presenting a genuine case to SSA in that regard, even if the evidence perhaps suggests otherwise. If you are presenting an honest case to SSA, even if you are not found disabled under the regulations, you are *not* committing fraud. Don't lie to doctors, or to the Judge. Do honestly tell them how you feel, and that you feel you are not able to do full time work. Even if objective testing suggests otherwise, if you truly believe what you are saying, then it's not fraud. If someone else thinks you are committing fraud by pursuing your disability claim, they are wrong. Fraud requires intent. If you do not intend to lie, it's not fraud. As I have said, those

232

are uninformed opinions from people who have no business weighing in on your disability claim. They simply don't matter. As long as you are pursuing your claim in good faith, which the vast majority of applicants are, there is no fraud.

This brings me to the next term, *waste*. While fraud is a very objective term with a very specific definition, waste is just the opposite. It is a highly subjective term. Is it *waste* to pay someone disability benefits? Is it *waste* to give someone who feels disabled due process and a fair hearing, even when the medical evidence strongly suggests the person would be able to do some type of full time work? One person's idea of *waste* is another person's idea of good government and a solid social safety net.

When someone talks about government *waste*, all that means is that the person does not agree with how those particular tax dollars are being spent. Some people think that Social Security Disability and other public benefits are a *waste* of money, while others think that spending trillions of dollars on foreign wars is a *waste* of money. This is a loaded term that people use when they disagree with the very concept of public benefits for someone who is disabled. If someone accuses you of *fraud*, and you are honestly pursuing your claim, that person is just wrong. But if someone accuses you of *waste*, that is an opinion that shows their values. Everyone is entitled to an opinion.

This bring us to the last term, *abuse*, which lies somewhere in between the objective term, *fraud,* and the subjective term, *waste*. Generally, whether one person's actions constitute an *abuse* of public resources is another person's opinion. Still, it is possible to engage in action that is objectively abusive of the system. For example, filing one, two, or even three disability applications may be seen as abusive, or it may be viewed as simply protecting one's right to pursue earned benefits. Yet by the 10th application, it's hard to argue with an allegation of abuse. At that point, we would probably all agree that person should stop filing applications and just move on with their life. That is obviously an extreme example, and such cases are admittedly rare. But I have seen cases where people will file a claim over and over with the same evidence. In my experience, this happens when unrepresented people are denied and quickly reapply, without obtaining new evidence to show that anything has changed.

I had a case once where the claimant told the Judge he did not recognize her authority, he refused to be sworn in so he could testify, and he walked out of the hearing room. That person, you might say, was *abusing* the process by filing a claim with no intention of fully participating. But perhaps that claimant filed the claim with the intent to cooperate, and then became disillusioned along the way. With two state agency denials, and a long delay before the hearing, you could see how this might occur.

Or perhaps this claimant was just having a bad day. Or perhaps he had a personality disorder, and that behavior was a symptom of his impairment. If that was the case, and the same behavior is what caused the claimant to be unable to work, does that change your opinion on whether he was *abusing* the system? In fact, his behavior at the hearing might actually corroborate evidence in the medical record if such behavior had occurred in the past, and the Judge could then approve the claim.

The point here is that when you hear a phrase such as "fraud, waste, and abuse," it's best to consider who is making that accusation, and what their motives are. Those who support a solid social safety net (taking care of people when they need help) and who want to strengthen Social Security's finances so SSA can continue to pay benefits to those who are entitled to receive them, are unlikely to use such a phrase. It is more likely to come from someone who cannot point to widespread *fraud*, who has a generalized yet unsupported opinion that SSA *wastes* money, and who has no idea how much *abuse* actually occurs. This is a political phrase, and for the most part, it's just opinion. As I said above, there are some isolated incidents of fraud, and when those do occur, people are prosecuted and penalized with large fines and even prison time, but such cases are rare.

Just because a case does not have the best evidence does not mean that SSA is being defrauded. Just because someone who alleges difficulty walking throughout the course of a 40 hour workweek is sometimes observed to be walking, does not mean that person should go to prison for trying to steal from the government. Social Security's process is not perfect, and the evidence is rarely perfect at proving a person to be very clearly disabled or very clearly not disabled.

This is why we have human Judges, who are asked to exercise judgment. As I have highlighted throughout this book, the system has its problems, and many of them should be closely examined by Congress and reformed. But ultimately, I do believe that most people applying for Social Security Disability benefits truly believe they are entitled to receive them, and the whole point of the process discussed throughout this book is to establish a medical basis for granting or denying those benefits. So, for those people who think Social Security is just a bunch of "fraud, waste, and abuse," well, like I said, they are entitled to their opinion, even when it's wrong.

If you are honestly pursuing a claim because you truly believe you are disabled and unable to work, there is no *fraud*. If you do not believe you are wasting anyone else's time with your application, then from your point of view, there is no *waste*. As long as you are following SSA's rules and procedures, you are not *abusing* the system. In fact, Congress is the one engaging in *waste* by forcing you to go through such an inefficient process. But you are not doing anything wrong. You are simply asserting your right to access benefits to which you are entitled. The process will be stressful enough without you worrying about things you cannot control, which includes what other people think. Focus on the things you can control, like receiving medical treatment and preparing for your hearing. That is the best use of your time and energy.

34. Fixing the System

Would government benefits be less *wasteful* if they could be given out with a lower overall cost to the taxpayers? If so, isn't it then *wasteful* to choose to hand out benefits in a way that is far more expensive? A Universal Basic Income (UBI) would be a much cheaper way to distribute government benefits, including disability benefits, so I believe it's very wasteful to use the system we have now instead of a UBI.

The basic idea of a UBI is that instead of the hodgepodge of government programs we have now, one simple universal payment would be automatically issued to everyone in the United States, without the need to prove anything to anyone. With a UBI, there would be no unemployment benefits, disability benefits, free/reduced lunch program, WIC (special supplemental nutrition program for women, infants, and children), SNAP (supplemental nutrition assistance program), TANF (temporary assistance for needy families), worker's compensation, subsidized housing, housing vouchers, etc. None of these programs, for which people have to apply and qualify, would be necessary. Instead, every American would receive a single UBI payment. Such a system would do away with the need to prove eligibility, and recipients would not be made to feel ashamed for receiving taxpayer funded public services.

Every person living in the United States benefits from public services – public schools, public roads, USDA inspected food, police, fire fighters, building codes, protection from the Army, etc. However, recipients of some services are told they should feel shame or stigma for using that particular service. Why is TANF called "temporary assistance for *needy* families?" Why is SNAP called "supplemental nutrition *assistance* program?" We don't call the Army "protection for *needy* people" or "protection *assistance* program." There is no reason why the use of any public service should come with shame or stigma.

This is why a UBI would be a better system for delivery of public benefits. There is no need to qualify for a UBI, so there is no stigma, as everyone would receive the benefit. This also means there would be no need for the enormous bureaucracy at the local, state, and federal levels to determine who qualifies and who doesn't. The bureaucracy necessary to administer all of these programs would disappear, saving billions of dollars annually. If you think this cannot work, consider that in 2020 and 2021, three such payments were distributed to almost every American. They were called "Economic Impact Payments," but most people just called them *stimulus* payments. They were authorized by Congress, paid by the Internal Revenue Service (IRS), and most Americans received them. No one applied for these payments, no evidence needed to be submitted, and no Judges were involved.

To me, this sounds like a far more efficient system, and certainly in 2020 and 2021, the Economic Impact Payments worked very well at helping people buy groceries and pay rent during the pandemic, something the world had not experienced in over 100 years. With a UBI, no one needs to qualify for anything, which also means no one needs to apply, hope, wait, hope some more, and then be denied benefits they feel they deserve and desperately need.

Under the current system, even when approved, a person needs to continue to qualify for the benefits, and often there is a review process to ensure the person continues to qualify. For example, after approving someone for disability benefits, Social Security conducts CDRs to make sure recipients continue to be disabled. If claimants improve medically, their benefits can and will be stopped.

But with a UBI, none of that would be necessary. When someone becomes unemployed, or disabled, there would be no need for that person to worry about paying rent or buying food. The luxuries of life may temporarily disappear as the family's income goes away, but the basics could be handled with no problem due to the UBI. Someone in that position could at least cover rent, utilities, and groceries. There would be no worry about that person becoming homeless, about the power being cut off, or about children going hungry.

There are additional positive effects that ripple throughout the economy. When someone has an address, a bed, and a shower, and when that person does not need to worry about how to feed or house their children, that person is far more likely to be able to apply for jobs, attend interviews, and ultimately the person is more employable. As soon as the person finds a job, that person starts paying taxes into the system again, which in turn pays for the UBI for that person and other people in similar circumstances. Because people get back to work faster, the economy does not spiral out of control and into a deep recession.

Thus, a UBI stops people from falling into a cycle of financial difficulty that is nearly impossible to break free from. Without a UBI, people in that situation often cannot buy food, cannot avoid having the power cut off, and cannot avoid being evicted. Throughout the pandemic, Congress and the 50 state legislatures had to step in and order rent relief, and relief for repayment of other loans, such as student loans. But that move negatively impacted landlords who invested in properties expecting to be paid rent, and other creditors who had loaned people money with the expectation that the loans would be repaid. Thus, this move, intended to help people in need, had a negative ripple effect throughout the economy. Instead of the positive ripple that we have with a UBI, we get a negative ripple that can lead to a prolonged recession as people stop spending money. What an awful system.

Also, when something like a pandemic does happen, Congress has to scramble to quickly get Economic Impact Payments out, to put rent relief in place, to pause student loan payments, etc. However, none of these things are done quickly, or well. If you lose your job today and you cannot pay your rent or buy groceries next week, Congress promising you a single $1,200 check six to eight weeks from now does not help...at all.

Also, we now know that the Paycheck Protection Program (PPP) put in place by Congress at the beginning of the pandemic did not help small businesses, low wage employees, or essential workers like it was supposed to. Instead, a lot of fraud occurred, and billions of dollars went to very large corporations because the program was created quickly and haphazardly. If, instead, every American already had a UBI coming their way, the PPP would not have been needed, the unemployment mess that happened throughout the pandemic would have been avoided, and Congress would not have spent six trillion dollars trying to avert a recession. A UBI would have been so much cheaper and more efficient.

In the case of someone who is disabled, with a UBI in place, the person can maintain a home, get necessary treatment, and potentially get back to full or part time work more quickly. On top of that, there is the added benefit of no Judges, no Attorney Advisor decision writers, and no Appeals Council. All of those costs can instead go into the UBI, to the actual taxpaying citizens who can actually use those payments for their own basic needs. A UBI makes

240

life simpler by providing a modest, dependable income to everyone, so they can satisfy their basic needs no matter what happens in their lives or in the world around them.

Yes, a UBI is a direct redistribution of wealth from the high income earners who pay a large portion of the income taxes to, well, everyone. But let's be honest, redistribution is happening anyway within all of the programs I listed above. With a UBI, the redistribution is just more efficient. There is no need to determine who qualifies and for how long. In other words, instead of redistributing to bureaucrats and recipients, the UBI redistributes only to recipients, with minimal employees needed to administer the program.

In this way, everyone benefits (well, except for the bureaucrats, such as the tens of thousands of employees who administer the Social Security Disability program at the national, regional, and local levels). Even if someone does not believe they need the money, they would still receive it. So, if those people ever do find that they are in a situation they never expected to be in (for example, a pandemic happens and a lot of people suddenly lose what seemed like very secure jobs), the UBI would be there for them too.

You may be asking yourself why I would be advocating for a UBI when I know that such a move would likely put my former colleagues out of business. In addition to the Attorney Advisors, the Administrative Law Judges, the other Social Security staff, and even claimant representatives would find themselves out of a job. But all of these people can relax. I do not foresee Congress creating a UBI anytime soon.

It would be far more efficient, but it's not the system we have in place. While it's great to consider how the administration of public benefits could be implemented more efficiently (*way* more efficiently!) in the United States, we ultimately have to understand the current system and how to navigate it, because for now, it's all we have.

Glossary

Administrative Appeals Judge (AAJ): The person at the Appeals Council who will review your appeal and decide whether to remand the case to the ALJ, issue a new decision, or allow the ALJ's decision to become final.

Administrative Law Judge (ALJ): The person at a hearing office who will conduct your hearing and issue a decision in your case.

Alleged Onset Date (AOD): This is the date that the claimant alleges disability began.

Appeals Council: This is the part of SSA that handles appeals from the ALJ/hearing level.

Appeals Officer: The person at the Appeals Council who will review your appeal and decide to deny your request for review or effectuate a favorable decision. If this person wishes to remand the case back to the ALJ or issue a new Appeals Council decision, the case will need to be sent to an AAJ.

Attorney Advisor: The attorney at a hearing office who will review the instructions from the ALJ and draft a decision in your case. Also known as an Attorney Advisor decision writer.

Attorney Analyst: The attorney at the Appeals Council who will review your appeal, draft an analysis for the AAJ or Appeals Officer to review, and who will also draft one of three things: (1) a letter explaining the basis for jurisdiction that will be mailed to you and your representative, (2) a remand order sending the case back to the ALJ, or (3) a new Appeals Council decision.

Basic Work Activities: The abilities and aptitudes necessary to do most jobs, and they include: walking, standing, sitting, lifting, pushing, pulling, reaching, carrying, handling, seeing, hearing, and speaking. These activities further include understanding, remembering, and carrying out simple instructions; making simple judgments; responding appropriately to supervision, co-workers, and usual work situations; and dealing with changes in a routine work setting.

Case Technicians: The hearing office staff who gather medical evidence, call claimants to schedule hearings, manage communication with representatives, and handle all of the other legwork that is required to open the case, complete the medical record, and make sure everything goes smoothly for the Judges and attorneys.

Code of Federal Regulations (CFR): The source of all federal regulations. Everything related to Social Security Disability is found at Title 20 of the CFR (Part 404 for SSDI regulations, and Part 416 for SSI regulations).

Commissioner of Social Security: This is the person in charge of the entire Social Security Administration, appointed by the President on the advice and consent of the U.S. Senate.

Congressional Inquiry: You can ask the office of your U.S. Representative or U.S. Senator to contact SSA and get a status update for your case. However, you will not have a hearing more quickly, and intervention by your member of Congress will not increase your odds of a favorable outcome.

Consultative Examiner: This doctor will see the claimant at the request of the state agency. The examination may be quick, around 10 minutes. This doctor will write a report, which will typically include a medical opinion explaining what activities the doctor believes you can do based on your medical records and the examination.

Continuing Disability Review: This happens when SSA reviews the case of someone who was found disabled to see if the person remains disabled.

Date Last Insured (DLI): This is the last date that you will be eligible for Title 2 benefits. Thus, you must be found disabled before this date to be eligible for these benefits. However, as you keep working and earning quarter credits, this date keeps moving out into the future. As a result, many people will never actually reach their DLI.

Disabled Adult Child (DAC): A Title 2 claim for a person whose disability begins between the ages of 18 and 22. This person files a claim on someone else's Social Security record, typically a parent/guardian. The record holder must be dead, disabled, or retired.

Disabled Widow's Benefits (DWB): A Title 2 claim for a person whose disability begins after age 50, if that person's spouse is deceased. This person files a claim on the Social Security record of the deceased spouse.

Duration Requirement: SSA defines disability as the inability to engage in substantial gainful activity (SGA) due to a medical impairment (or impairments) for a period of at least 12 continuous months. The 12 month period is called the "duration requirement" because it represents the duration for which a person has to be impaired to qualify for Social Security Disability benefits (SSDI or SSI).

Established Onset Date (EOD): This is the date that the Judge finds disability began. This may be different from the Alleged Onset Date.

Federal Court: *See United States District Court*

Fee Agreement: The way most disability representatives want to be paid. The agreement is signed by the claimant and the representative. It will explain that the representative's fee is capped at 25% of the past due benefits, up to a limit that is currently set by Congress at $6,000 (increasing to $7,200 in November 2022). The agreement may also explain that the representative can collect a minimal amount for costs incurred, such as making photocopies, printing documents, and obtaining the claimant's medical records. The Judge must review and approve the fee agreement to make sure it follows all SSA rules.

Fee Petition: An alternative way for disability representatives to be paid. The representative will need to provide SSA with information regarding how much time was spent on the case to justify why there should be a fee. This method can be used instead of a fee agreement, but is most often used when there is no valid fee agreement in place. For example, if the claimant has signed a fee agreement with another representative, who refuses to waive their right to collect a fee, then a new representative can only be paid by filing a fee petition.

FICA tax: This payroll tax combines the employer and employee portions of both the OASDI tax and the Medicare tax. Currently, the total of all portions is 15.3%.

Five-Step Sequential Evaluation: *See Sequential Evaluation Process.*

Fiscal Year: This is how the United States government measures time. The U.S. fiscal year begins on October 1st each year, and ends on September 30th of the following year.

Fully Insured: This means you have acquired 40 quarter credits throughout your life. Once acquired, you will never lose this status. The requirements for people under age 31 are less stringent because those people have had less time during their lives to work and earn credits.

Group Supervisor: A middle manager within a hearing office. This person supervises Attorney Advisors and Case Technicians.

Heavy work: Work that mostly involves standing or walking, for up to six hours per eight hour workday. May also involve lifting or carrying up to 100 pounds occasionally and 50 pounds frequently. May also involve bending or stooping frequently. While defined in SSA regulations, this term is almost never used by Judges in hearings or in decisions.

Hearing Office Chief Administrative Law Judge (HOCALJ): The highest-ranking SSA staff member at a hearing office. Oversees all of the Judges and the management team.

Hearing Office Director (HOD): The manager at a hearing office who supervises the Group Supervisors. The highest ranking member of a hearing office management team. Overseen by the Hearing Office Chief Administrative Law Judge.

Initial Review: The first level of review of a disability application. This review is completed by the state agency of the claimant's state of residence.

Light work: Work that mostly involves standing or walking, for up to six hours per eight hour workday. May also involve lifting or carrying up to 20 pounds occasionally and 10 pounds frequently. May also involve bending or stooping, but only occasionally.

Medicaid: A public health insurance program for people with low income that is financed by a combination of state and federal funding.

Medicare: A public health insurance program that mostly serves people over the age of 65. However, a person found disabled and eligible for Title 2 benefits can become eligible for Medicare before age 65. Medicare carries a 30 month waiting period following the EOD, during which you will not receive Medicare coverage.

Medical Expert: This is a doctor who may be called to testify at your hearing. This doctor may review your medical records and discuss your physical impairments or your mental impairments. The doctor will typically also provide a medical opinion explaining what activities the doctor believes you can do based on your medical records.

Medicare Qualified Government Employee (MQGE): This type of claim is utilized by some local government employees, like teachers, who pay into a pension, and do not pay the OASDI tax. This claim is for Medicare coverage only, no monetary benefits are involved. The claimant must be found disabled under all the same rules as if they had filed an SSDI claim.

Medicare tax: This payroll tax funds Medicare for persons over 65 and also for qualifying SSDI recipients. Employees pay 1.45% and their employers pay 1.45%.

Medium work: Work that mostly involves standing or walking, for up to six hours per eight hour workday. May also involve lifting or carrying up to 50 pounds occasionally and 25 pounds frequently. May also involve bending or stooping frequently.

OASDI tax: This tax, for Old-Age, Survivors, and Disability insurance, is a payroll tax. Employees pay 6.2% and their employers pay 6.2%. This tax funds the Social Security trust fund that pays retirement benefits, disability insurance benefits, and survivor's benefits.

Overpayment: This happens when SSA accidentally pays you too much in benefits, or benefits to which you were not entitled, and wants them back.

Over Resourced: This happens when an SSI applicant/recipient has too many assets or too much income to become/remain eligible for SSI.

Past Relevant Work (PRW): This is work that you have done during the past 15 years, that you performed at the SGA level, and which was done long enough to have learned to do it to an average performance level.

Preponderance of the Evidence: The standard for proving a Social Security Disability claim. The claimant must show that it is "more likely than not" that the person has a medical impairment or impairments that prevents the ability to engage in SGA for a continuous period of 12 months.

Program Operations Manual System (POMS): A manual that provides guidance to SSA staff regarding how to apply the rules and regulations of the entire Social Security program.

Quarter Credits: These are earned by working and paying the OASDI tax. One credit is earned for every $1,510 that is earned during the year, up to a maximum of four credits, regardless of when during the year the income is earned.

Reconsideration: The second level of review of a disability application, also at the state agency. This level applies in 40 of the 50 states. However, 10 states bypass this level of review: Alabama, Alaska, parts of California, Colorado, Louisiana, Michigan, Missouri, New Hampshire, New York, and Pennsylvania.

Remand: This is when a case is reversed on appeal and sent back to the level it had been to previously. Typically, a Social Security Disability case will be remanded either by the Appeals Council or by the United States District Court, and sent back to the hearing level for a new hearing with an ALJ. The ALJ will hold a new hearing and issue a new decision.

Representative: An attorney or non-attorney who provides counsel to a Social Security claimant and appears with that person at their hearing.

Representative Payee: A person who manages Social Security benefits on someone else's behalf when that person cannot manage benefits in their own best interest.

Request For Review: The name for an appeal to the Appeals Council.

Residual Functional Capacity (RFC): The is a determination of the *most* you can do despite your medical impairments.

Sedentary work: Work that mostly involves sitting down. May involve standing or walking for up to two hours per eight hour workday. May also involve lifting or carrying up to 10 pounds.

Sequential Evaluation Process: The process SSA uses to determine that a person is disabled. While there are only five official steps to the process, there are actually six or seven steps depending on whether you have an SSDI claim or an SSI claim.

Severe Impairment: Any physical or mental impairment that more than minimally impacts any basic work activity for a period of 12 continuous months. In legal terms, we call this a *de minimus* test because it is a very low bar and therefore very easy to meet this standard.

Social Security Administration (SSA): The federal agency that administers the retirement and disability benefits programs in the United States.

Social Security Disability Insurance (SSDI): Benefits under Title 2 of the Social Security Act. Also called disability insurance benefits, DIB, Title 2 benefits, or simply SSDI. You qualify for these benefits by paying the OASDI tax and earning quarter credits. SSDI carries a five month waiting period following the EOD, during which you will not receive any benefits.

Specific Vocational Preparation (SVP): The way SSA determines the precise amount of time a person needs to have done a job to have learned to do it to an average performance level. Unskilled occupations have an SVP level 1 or 2. Semi-skilled occupations have an SVP level 3 or 4. Skilled occupations have an SVP level 5 through 9.

State agency medical consultant: The claimant will never meet this doctor. At the request of the state agency, this doctor will review all of the claimant's medical records, and will author a report. The report will typically also include a medical opinion explaining what activities the doctor believes you can do based on your medical records.

Substantial Gainful Activity (SGA): You must be earning less than this amount to qualify for SSDI or SSI benefits. In 2022, the amount is $1,350 per month. This amount typically increases by a small amount each year.

Supplemental Security Income (SSI): Benefits under Title 16 of the Social Security Act. These benefits are funded by regular income taxes, and this program has strict income and asset limits.

Substantial Evidence: The standard of review on appeal for a Social Security Disability case. The Appeals Council or the United States District Court will decide whether there is "more than a mere scintilla of evidence" to support the findings in the ALJ's decision.

Substitute Party: The person who will receive benefits on the claimant's behalf if the claimant passes away before an award of benefits. This may also be the legal representative of the claimant's estate (for Title 2 claims), or the state in which the claimant lived (for Title 16 claims).

Transferability of Skills: This is a type of Step 5 denial. If you have skilled past relevant work, the Judge can find that you have acquired some skills doing that work that would transfer to other work that exists in significant numbers in the national economy, and then deny your claim.

Trial Work Period (TWP): A program that allows SSDI recipients to try and go back to work. During the TWP, if a recipient earns more than a certain amount nine months out of 60, the TWP will end. In 2022, this amount is $970 per month, and it typically increases by a small amount each year.

United States District Court ("Federal Court"): After the Appeals Council denies your request for review, if you still wish to appeal further, this is where you would need to take your case next.

Universal Basic Income (UBI): A program that gives one monthly payment to every United States resident. This would, in theory, replace all other public benefits programs, and be a more efficient and effective social safety net.

Unsuccessful Work Attempt (UWA): An effort to do work in employment or self-employment that ends, or reduces to below the SGA level, within six months. The reduction in earnings must be due to the claimant's medical impairment(s) or the removal of special conditions related to those impairment(s). Work performed during a UWA does not prevent a finding of disability because it does not disrupt 12 continuous months under SGA.

Vocational Expert: A jobs expert who will testify at the hearing. This person will evaluate specific work related limitations and state whether someone with those limitations can do the claimant's past relevant work or other work that exists in significant numbers in the national economy.